# Pass It On
## at SCHOOL!

## Activity Handouts for
## Creating Caring Schools

# BY JEANNE ENGELMANN

| Search | Practical research |
|--------|--------------------|
| INSTITUTE | benefiting children and youth |

*Pass It On at School! Activity Handouts for Creating Caring Schools* is a resource of Search Institute's Healthy Communities • Healthy Youth initiative. This effort seeks to unite individuals, organizations, and communities to join together in nurturing competent, caring, and responsible children and adolescents. The founding national sponsor for Healthy Communities • Healthy Youth is Thrivent Financial for Lutherans, a nonprofit fraternal benefit society providing financial services and community service opportunities for Lutherans nationwide.

**About Search Institute**
Search Institute is an independent, nonprofit, nonsectarian organization whose mission is to provide leadership, knowledge, and resources to promote healthy children, youth and communities. The institute collaborates with others to promote long-term organizational and cultural change that supports its mission. For a free information packet, call 800-888-7828.

**Pass It On at School! Activity Handouts for Creating Caring Schools**
**Jeanne Engelmann**

Copyright © 2003 by Search Institute

At the time of this book's publication, all facts and figures cited are the most current available; all telephone numbers, addresses, and Web site URLs are accurate and active; all publications, organizations, Web sites, and other resources exist as described in this book; and all efforts have been made to verify them. The author and Search Institute make no warranty or guarantee concerning the information and materials given out by organizations or content found at Web sites, and we are not responsible for any changes that occur after this book's publication. If you find an error or believe that a resource listed here is not as described, please contact Client Services at Search Institute.

10  9  8  7  6  5  4  3  2

**Search Institute**
615 First Avenue Northeast, Suite 125
Minneapolis, MN 55413
www.search-institute.org
612-376-8955
800-888-7828

**Credits**
**Editors:** Kalisha Davis, Kay Hong, Susan Wichman
**Production Manager:** Mary Ellen Buscher
**Design:** Christian Fünfhausen

**Library of Congress Cataloging-in-Publication Data**
Engelmann, Jeanne
    Pass it on at school! : activity handouts for creating caring schools / Jeanne Engelmann.
      p. cm.
   ISBN: 1-57482-835-5
   1. School improvement programs--United States.  2. School environment--United States.  3. Activity
   programs in education--United States.  4. Communication in education--United States.  I. Title.
LB2822.82.E55 2003
371.7--dc21

                   2003007387

**Licensing and Copyright**
The handouts in *Pass It On at School! Activity Handouts for Creating Caring Schools* may be copied as many times for as many people as you want. We ask that each time you copy one of them, you respect the following guidelines: Search Institute credit and copyright information on each handout is not removed, altered, or obscured in reproduction. Any material added for local distribution is clearly differentiated from material prepared by Search Institute. Search Institute material is not altered in content or meaning. The handouts are not resold for profit. You may use the information from the handouts in other formats for promotional or educational purposes, using the following attribution: Reprinted with permission from *Pass It On at School! Activity Handouts for Creating Caring Schools* (specify the number of the handout you are quoting) © 2003 by Search Institute, Minneapolis, Minnesota, 800-888-7828, www.search-institute.org. All rights reserved.

**Printing Tips**
These handouts will be more effective at getting the word out about asset building if the copies you distribute are neat and easy to read. Here are some things you can do to get high quality reproduction without spending a lot of money:
- Always copy from the original. Copying from a copy lowers the reproduction quality.
- Make copies more appealing by using brightly colored paper or even colored ink. Often a quick-print shop will have daily specials on certain colors of ink.
- Consider printing each handout on a different color paper for variety.
- If you are using more than one handout or a handout that is more than one page, make two-sided copies.
- Make sure the paper weight is heavy enough so that the words don't bleed through. We recommend using at least 60-pound offset paper. A 20-pound paper could show through.

# CONTENTS

There are 75 handouts grouped into 12 sections. Below is a list of each section and handout.

## In the Classroom (22–37)

## In the Staff Meeting (38–41)

## In the Cafeteria (42–44)

## In the Staff Lounge (45–47)

# PASS IT ON **AT SCHOOL!**

## In the Principal's Office (48-51)

## On the School Bus (52-53)

## In the Nurse's Office (54-55)

## In the Guidance Office (56-63)

## In the Locker Room/On the Field (64-67)

# Handouts Grouped for Specific Roles

Here is a guide that will help you find handouts for specific school staff like teachers, nurses, office staff, and principals. This listing may help you find what you need more quickly.

## Handouts for School Staff

### ALL SCHOOL STAFF

### TEACHERS AND SPECIAL EDUCATION STAFF

### GUIDANCE COUNSELORS, SOCIAL WORKERS, AND PREVENTION SPECIALISTS

## Handouts for Specific Grades

## TRANSITION PROGRAMS
### (FROM GRADES 6 TO 7 AND 8 TO 9)

## Handouts for Building Awareness and Support

### STUDENTS

### PARENT LEADERS AND ORGANIZATIONS

# INTRODUCTION

Welcome to *Pass It On at School! Activity Handouts for Creating Caring Schools*. This resource was created to help schools become better places for everyone who plays a role in the life of the school community. This book is a sequel to the popular *Pass It On! Ready-to-Use Handouts for Asset Builders* and, just like the original, this publication offers a variety of concrete suggestions for building assets with and for young people.

Whether you're just becoming familiar with the developmental assets framework or you're a seasoned asset builder, this book will make it easy for you to integrate asset building into your everyday work. The activity handouts in this book will help you reach other members of your school community, including teachers, administrators, guidance counselors, other school staff, students, parent and volunteer groups, and office and custodial staff. This book is designed so you can easily copy and distribute activity handouts during meetings and special presentations or create packets of information for groups that already exist. There is one important concept to remember as you begin to work with this resource: Everyone has the ability to be an asset builder!

And it takes everyone. Why? Schools face tremendous pressures to increase academic achievement and to meet state standards, as well as to deal with drugs, violence, and other social and health problems. As you well know, doing just one is hard enough, but to do all these things is almost impossible. Asset building can help make

healthy school climate more possible by bringing everyone together (not just principals and teachers) to make an important impact on the school environment. Every young person and adult (including parents/guardians) has the power to positively influence school environment.

The developmental assets framework is not a curriculum or program, but a way of thinking—a set of attitudes that encourage us to see what is right with children and adolescents. It gives us a way to re-evaluate our relationships with students. Think of the assets as the opportunities, skills, relationships, and values that form the building blocks for helping young people succeed.

## What Is an "Activity Handout"?

"Activity handout" is a term you will find throughout this publication and it implies that many of these activities may require some additional planning on behalf of the user to be successful. As the reader, you are encouraged to adapt these ideas as you see fit. This includes creating an activity that relates to the information presented or integrating the handouts into school activities that already exist. Resources and tips have been included throughout to help you imagine the possibilities.

## HOW TO USE THIS BOOK

The ideas and suggestions in this book will appeal to people who are a part of a school community. Some activity handouts are designed for school staff, some for various grade levels, some for students, and some for parents. For ease of use, the activity handouts are grouped by where the suggested activities will most likely take place:

- In the school building
- In the classroom
- In the the staff meeting
- In the staff lounge
- In the cafeteria
- In the principal's office
- On the school bus
- In the nurse's office
- In the guidance office
- In the locker room/on the field
- In parent meetings
- Outside the school (community partnerships)

Each activity handout includes at least two pages. The first page, labeled "Tips for Using," serves as a guide for using the material. It includes helpful information to keep in mind or use as talking points in presentation/group settings and practical ideas for how best to use the handout, such as the setting, audience, and materials needed. Next follows the companion handout that can be copied and distributed. We've included proper credit line information on each handout, so feel free to use them as often as you like. (See page ii for more information regarding licensing and copyright.)

Remember, these activity handouts are only suggestions—you can and should adapt them to fit your specific students, situations, groups, and classrooms. Everyone learns and understands her or his world in different ways. All of the activities suggested in this book can be adapted to a variety of learning styles when you:

- Encourage students (or adults) to work in small groups or pairs;

- Use art or stories to express opinions and ideas about a particular topic;
- Ask people to participate in role playing;
- Find ways to incorporate other media such as film, books, video, and computers; and
- Use music and/or movement to facilitate activities.

## THE ASSET MODEL

In an effort to promote the elements of a strength-based approach to healthy development, Search Institute developed the framework of developmental assets. This framework identifies 40 critical factors for young people's growth and development. When drawn together, the assets offer a set of relationships, opportunities, skills, and values that are critical to positive child and adolescent development. This list of assets reflects the important roles that families, peers, schools, congregations, neighborhoods, youth organizations, and others in communities play in shaping young people's lives.

The first four asset categories focus on external structures, relationships, and activities that create a positive environment for young people:

**Support**—Young people need to be surrounded by people who love, care for, appreciate, and accept them.

**Empowerment**—Young people need to feel valued and valuable. This happens when youth feel safe and respected.

**Boundaries and Expectations**—Young people need clear rules, consistent consequences for breaking rules, and encouragement to do their best.

**Constructive Use of Time**—Young people need opportunities—outside of school—to learn and develop new skills and interests with other youth and adults.

A community's responsibility for its young people does not end with the provision of external assets. There needs to be a similar commitment to nurturing the internal qualities that guide choices and create a sense of centeredness, purpose, and focus. Four categories of internal assets are included in the framework:

**Commitment to Learning**—Young people need a sense of the lasting importance of learning and a belief in their own abilities.

**Positive Values**—Young people need to develop strong guiding values or principles to help them make healthy life choices.

**Social Competencies**—Young people need the skills to interact effectively with others, to make difficult decisions, and to cope with new situations.

**Positive Identity**—Young people need to believe in their own self-worth and to feel that they have control over the things that happen to them.

## THE POWER OF ASSETS

The 40 developmental assets represent everyday wisdom about positive experiences and characteristics that can lead to the healthy development of all young people. Search Institute research reveals that these assets are powerful influences on adolescent behavior, evident across all cultural and socioeconomic groups of youth. Young people who report having more assets are less likely to exhibit problem behaviors and more likely to have a positive attitude about school.

Yet, while the assets can help shape a young person's life and choices, too few youth experience enough of them. The average young person surveyed reports experiencing only 19 of the 40 as-

sets. Overall, 66 percent of young people surveyed experience fewer than 20 of the assets. These data suggest more can be done to ensure that all youth grow into caring, responsible adults.

## BUILDING ASSETS WITH AND FOR STUDENTS

School is where many youth form friendships, connect with caring adults, and learn to use their time well, follow rules, and meet expectations. School is also an important place for young people to further develop values and social competencies. The activity handouts in this book will help busy administrators, teachers, and other school staff—indeed, everyone in the school community—build developmental assets with and for students.

What's the benefit? When young people experience a healthy school climate, their attitudes about ensuring a productive school community overall can change for the better. Youth need a key role in building a better school and can serve as valuable leaders in this effort by bringing other youth (and adults) on board and by pinpointing areas that need the most improvement. Adults willing to share this effort with students help bridge the generation gap and build a better school.

## GETTING THE WHOLE SCHOOL ON BOARD WITH ASSET BUILDING

At a time when many people feel overwhelmed by the problems and challenges facing children and adolescents, schools across the country are discovering new energy in working together toward a positive vision for young people. Instead of focusing solely on reducing risks and intervening in problems, these schools are rallying

---

To learn more about the assets—what they are and the difference they make in the lives of students—see the first two handouts, "Assets: What Are They?" and "The Asset-Building Difference."

to build the foundation of development that all young people need.

Uniting a school to nurture the positive development of students is a challenging, yet worthwhile goal. Every individual needs to feel encouraged to be an advocate for positive change. A school community can accomplish this when everyone —from the school board, principal, and teachers to support staff and students—is motivated and equipped to join together.

This effort usually begins with the vision of one or two people who understand the value of asset building. Positive change doesn't take an army, just a few caring people who want to see youth thrive.

How can a school community begin to address these needs? Six key principles can help guide any asset-building effort:

1. **Everyone can build assets.** Building assets isn't just about great families or schools or neighborhoods. It requires consistent messages across a community.

2. **All young people need assets.** While it is crucial to pay special attention to youth who struggle—economically, emotionally, or otherwise—nearly all young people need more assets than they have.

3. **Relationships are key.** Strong relationships between adults and young people, young people and their peers, and teenagers and children are central to asset building.

4. **Asset building is an ongoing process.** Building assets starts when a child is born and continues through high school and beyond.

5. **Consistent messages are important.** It is important for families, schools, communities, the media, and others to all give young people consistent and similar messages about what is important and what is expected of them.

6. **Intentional repetition is important.** Assets must be continually reinforced across the years and in all areas of a young person's life.

Promote these principles in your school by taking steps such as:

- Creating asset-building task forces within each area or building of the school;
- Encouraging your school board to pass a resolution that supports asset building;
- Supporting the administration of the *Search Institute Profiles of Student Life: Attitudes and Behaviors* survey in your district;
- Including asset-building information in each school newsletter;
- Educating parents or guardians about the assets;
- Sharing the asset-building model with coaches and extracurricular staff; and
- Using assignments, class discussions, and instructional projects to promote asset building.

This is just the short list. Let your imagination guide your steps in your own situation.

---

To help you begin the work of changing the climate of your school, see handout 10, "Schoolwide Asset-Building Project," for ideas. To learn more about connecting assets to curriculum and instruction, refer to *Powerful Teaching: Developmental Assets in Curriculum and Instruction,* available from Search Institute. For more information, visit our Web site: www.search-institute.org .

# IN THE SCHOOL BUILDING

# ASSETS: WHAT ARE THEY?

**KEY USER/S**
Teachers, administrators, parent organizations, student organizations

**ASSET CATEGORY**
All

**ASSETS ADDRESSED**
All

## KEEP THIS IN MIND

Some young people with all the advantages have problems as they grow up and others who grow up in harder circumstances succeed beautifully. Why? Search Institute set out to learn what helps some young people thrive in spite of difficulties. In an effort to promote the elements of a strength-based approach to healthy development, Search Institute developed the framework of developmental assets. This framework identifies 40 critical factors for young people's growth and development. When drawn together, the assets offer a set of relationships, opportunities, skills, and values that are critically related to positive child and adolescent development. The assets clearly show important roles that families, schools, congregations, neighborhoods, youth organizations, and others in communities play in shaping young people's lives.

## HOW TO USE THIS HANDOUT

The handout contains a list of all 40 assets. Here's what you might say to young people or adults: "These assets are divided into eight broad categories of human development that will help you think about the big picture and ways to address the whole child. Make copies to post in the classroom, staff lounge, office, cafeteria, and restrooms. As a personal reminder, you might also post the list on your bathroom mirror at home, on the dashboard of your car, in your locker, or on your classroom desk. Study the list and try pinpointing a few assets that you would like to build with and for students."

## NOTES:

For more information on how assets relate to schools, see handout 3, "Asset Power."

# ASSETS: WHAT ARE THEY?

## SEARCH INSTITUTE'S 40 DEVELOPMENTAL ASSETS

Search Institute has identified the following building blocks of healthy development that help young people grow up healthy, caring, and responsible.

## EXTERNAL ASSETS

### SUPPORT

1. **Family support**—Family life provides high levels of love and support.
2. **Positive family communication**—Young person and her or his parent(s) communicate positively, and young person is willing to seek advice and counsel from parent(s).
3. **Other adult relationships**—Young person receives support from three or more non-parent adults.
4. **Caring neighborhood**—Young person experiences caring neighbors.
5. **Caring school climate**—School provides a caring, encouraging environment.
6. **Parent involvement in schooling**—Parent(s) are actively involved in helping young person succeed in school.

### EMPOWERMENT

7. **Community values youth**—Young person perceives that adults in the community value youth.
8. **Youth as resources**—Young people are given useful roles in the community.
9. **Service to others**—Young person serves in the community one hour or more per week.
10. **Safety**—Young person feels safe at home, at school, and in the neighborhood.

### BOUNDARIES AND EXPECTATIONS

11. **Family boundaries**—Family has clear rules and consequences and monitors the young person's whereabouts.
12. **School boundaries**—School provides clear rules and consequences.
13. **Neighborhood boundaries**—Neighbors take responsibility for monitoring young people's behavior.
14. **Adult role models**—Parent(s) and other adults model positive, responsible behavior.
15. **Positive peer influence**—Young person's best friends model responsible behavior.
16. **High expectations**—Both parent(s) and teachers encourage the young person to do well.

### CONSTRUCTIVE USE OF TIME

17. **Creative activities**—Young person spends three or more hours per week in lessons or practice in music, theater, or other arts.

18. **Youth programs**—Young person spends three or more hours per week in sports, clubs, or organizations at school and/or in the community.
19. **Religious community**—Young person spends one or more hours per week in activities in a religious institution.
20. **Time at home**—Young person is out with friends "with nothing special to do" two or fewer nights per week.

# INTERNAL ASSETS
## COMMITMENT TO LEARNING

21. **Achievement motivation**—Young person is motivated to do well in school.
22. **School engagement**—Young person is actively engaged in learning.
23. **Homework**—Young person reports doing at least one hour of homework every school day.
24. **Bonding to school**—Young person cares about her or his school.
25. **Reading for pleasure**—Young person reads for pleasure three or more hours per week.

## POSITIVE VALUES

26. **Caring**—Young person places high value on helping other people.
27. **Equality and social justice**—Young person places high value on promoting equality and reducing hunger and poverty.
28. **Integrity**—Young person acts on convictions and stands up for her or his beliefs.

29. **Honesty**—Young person "tells the truth even when it is not easy."
30. **Responsibility**—Young person accepts and takes personal responsibility.
31. **Restraint**—Young person believes it is important not to be sexually active or to use alcohol or other drugs.

## SOCIAL COMPETENCIES

32. **Planning and decision making**—Young person knows how to plan ahead and make choices.
33. **Interpersonal competence**—Young person has empathy, sensitivity, and friendship skills.
34. **Cultural competence**—Young person has knowledge of and comfort with people of different cultural/racial/ethnic backgrounds.
35. **Resistance skills**—Young person can resist negative peer pressure and dangerous situations.
36. **Peaceful conflict resolution**—Young person seeks to resolve conflict nonviolently.

## POSITIVE IDENTITY

37. **Personal power**—Young person feels he or she has control over "things that happen to me."
38. **Self-esteem**—Young person reports having a high self-esteem.
39. **Sense of purpose**—Young person reports that "my life has a purpose."
40. **Positive view of personal future**—Young person is optimistic about her or his personal future.

# THE ASSET-BUILDING DIFFERENCE

**KEY USER/S**
Teachers, administrators, parent organizations, student organizations

**ASSET CATEGORY**
All

**ASSETS ADDRESSED**
All

## KEEP THIS IN MIND

The 40 developmental assets are 40 opportunities, skills, relationships, values, qualities and self-perceptions that all young people need to succeed. Using the assets to make a difference in the lives of students requires some basic shifts in our thinking. In order to build a school community in which students feel connected, engaged, and responsible, we must be committed to the asset principles and willing to change our thinking.

## HOW TO USE THIS HANDOUT

This handout serves as an easy tool to explain the shift in thinking the assets ask adults to make about young people.

Use this handout:

- As a personal checklist to remind you and fellow staff members to replace old attitudes with asset-building perceptions, language, and actions;

- At small group sessions for school staff, including school bus drivers, food service workers, and custodians; and

- To raise awareness among school board members and other administrative staff.

If you use this handout during a workshop or staff meeting, ask participants to add their own ideas. Post this expanded list in key areas of the school, such as the staff lounge or office.

## NOTES:

# THE ASSET-BUILDING DIFFERENCE

**The asset-building difference helps us focus on positive thoughts and actions when we:**

| MOVE FROM . . . | TO . . . |
|---|---|
| Viewing students as problems | Seeing students as resources |
| Talking about problems | Talking about possibilities and positives |
| Reacting to problems | Actively building strengths |
| Treating students as objects of teaching | Respecting students as actors in their own development |
| Relying on professionals to help | Involving everyone in the lives of students |
| Managing crises | Building a shared vision |
| Focusing on troubled students | Focusing on all students |
| Blaming others | Claiming personal responsibility |
| Competing priorities | Cooperative efforts |
| Conflicting signals about values and priorities | Consistent messages about what is important |

# PASS IT ON **AT SCHOOL!**

TIPS FOR USING **Activity Handout 3**

# ASSET POWER

**KEY USER/S**
All school staff

**ASSET CATEGORY**
All

**ASSETS ADDRESSED**
All

## KEEP THIS IN MIND

What's so important about assets? Why bother with asset building? From Search Institute's extensive youth surveys conducted in the United States and Canada, we know that the more assets students experience, the more likely they are to report success in school and report having a positive outlook on the future. Students are also less likely to report engaging in risky behavior. A quick summary:

- Students who report higher levels of assets also report decreased levels of high-risk behaviors such as alcohol and other drug use, early sexual activity, and violence.

- Assets are related to reports of increased levels of positive attitudes and behavior and to helping students delay gratification, value diversity, succeed in school, and maintain good health.

School staff members can work to build assets through positive interaction and by supporting a healthy school climate.

## HOW TO USE THIS HANDOUT

Of the 40 assets, more than half have a direct impact on school success. Use the handout to show others the benefits of asset building. Encourage staff members to review the information and ask them: "Are any of these percentages surprising? Which particular assets do you think you might be able to focus on in your work?"

Here are some additional talking points:

- Schools can have a direct impact on more than half the developmental assets, including the 13 assets Search Institute researchers suggest are very important in promoting academic success.

- Only 7 of the 22 developmental assets Search Institute reports schools can directly influence are experienced by half or more of students.

- The majority of the key developmental assets related to academic success involve relationships more than they do programs. These data show that only a minority of students experience school as a caring place—where students care about each other and where students get care and encouragement from their teachers.

Such conversations can be great motivation to help students develop assets. The handout can also be used in small staff workshops or as a way to generate support from school board members. Make copies to distribute or make an overhead that can be kept in front of your audience as you make the case for asset building.

# ASSET POWER

Why bother with asset building in your school? Let the numbers speak! The following shows 22 assets that schools can most directly affect.

## ASSETS SCHOOLS CAN AFFECT

## % OF YOUTH EXPERIENCING ASSET

| Asset | % |
|---|---|
| Achievement motivation* | 67 |
| Positive peer influence* | 65 |
| School engagement* | 61 |
| Youth programs* | 58 |
| Bonding to school* | 54 |
| School boundaries* | 53 |
| Homework* | 53 |
| Safety | 51 |
| Service to others | 51 |
| High expectations* | 49 |
| Interpersonal competence* | 47 |
| Other adult relationships* | 45 |
| Peaceful conflict resolution | 45 |
| Resistance skills | 42 |
| Parent involvement in schooling* | 34 |
| Planning and decision making | 30 |
| Adult role models | 30 |
| Caring school climate* | 29 |
| Youth as resources | 28 |
| Community values youth | 25 |
| Reading for pleasure* | 23 |
| Creative activities | 20 |

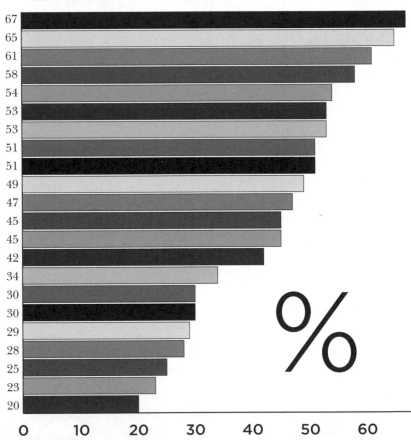

*Assets that research suggests are most important to academic success. Statistics from 1999–2000 school year surveys of 217,277 students grades 6–12 in public and private U.S. schools.

Percentages of young people who report experiencing each asset were gathered from the *Search Institute Profiles of Student Life: Attitudes and Behaviors* survey in 318 communities and 33 states.

# BUILD ASSETS TOGETHER

**KEY USER/S**
Students

**ASSET CATEGORY**
Boundaries and Expectations,
Constructive Use of Time

**ASSETS ADDRESSED**
#15, Positive Peer Influence
#18, Youth Programs

## KEEP THIS IN MIND

Many students are already actively engaged in the life of the school or have an interest in something that the school community might benefit from. Tap into their energy, resourcefulness, and connection with other students to build assets. Schools can help students figure out ways to build specific assets within the context of team, club, or other group activities. Make sure to build in a way to recognize goals accomplished and reward successes.

## HOW TO USE THIS HANDOUT

Gather students together and talk with them about how much influence they have with their peers. Distribute the list of developmental assets (Activity Handout 1) and describe the framework. Ask students to name two assets their group already has going for it and to select two they'd like their team, club, or other group to focus on. Then brainstorm ways young people can help their peers

develop the selected assets. Copy and distribute the handout to help students record their thoughts, goals, and action steps—something to take away with them when the meeting is over.

Listed below are some basic facts in simple language that can help you as your group begins to talk about the assets.

The 40 developmental assets are:

- A list of things that help young people to be healthy, caring, and productive.
- Things everyone can do or build in the community.
- Things every young person deserves to have in her or his life. Some are inside of you, but some come from parents or guardians, teachers, friends, and relatives.
- Things that can make a positive difference in your life.
- Based on the relationships you have with your family, friends, and other people.
- The things that can help young people live a better life and be more successful.
- The relationships, opportunities, and self-perceptions that can help you make dreams come true. (When you feel good about yourself, you're more likely to want to do well in school, to look for friends who treat you with respect, and to think positively about your future.)
- Building blocks that can help you become the kind of man or woman you want to be.

# BUILD ASSETS TOGETHER

Take a few minutes to write (or draw) ideas that you have about building assets for yourself and other students in our school community. Where are we now? What can the future look like?

**My team/club/group already has these strengths:**

*Example: The members of our basketball team really care about each other and about the school.*

1. _____

2. _____

3. _____

**We could be better if we worked to develop these assets:**

*Example: Our theater club would have better performances if we took more personal responsibility for being on time for rehearsals and if we supported each other through our words and actions.*

1. _____

2. _____

3. _____

**These are my ideas for helping my group strengthen the assets I listed above:**

*Example: I can suggest to the academic games adviser that we set up a reward for the team members who consistently show up on time for every practice. I can also offer my best tips/strategies to help my teammates become positive peer influences and ask others to do the same.*

1. _____

2. _____

3. _____

PASS IT ON **AT SCHOOL!** ——————————
TIPS FOR USING **Activity Handout 5**

# STUDENT SYMPOSIUM QUESTIONNAIRE

**KEY USER/S**
Students

**ASSET CATEGORY**
Empowerment, Boundaries and Expectations

**ASSETS ADDRESSED**
#8, Youth as Resources
#9, Service to Others
#15, Positive Peer Influence

## KEEP THIS IN MIND

Place power and influence squarely into the hands of students by inviting them to brainstorm ways to build awareness about the assets among peers. One great way to reach out to students and encourage their creative thinking is to sponsor a student-led, schoolwide conference. This type of activity will take the cooperation of various staff members, including the principal, especially if such a conference takes place during school hours.

In the Fox Cities of Wisconsin, young people collaborated to offer a similar event. Here's their story.

## Teen Symposium in the Fox Cities of Wisconsin

PAUL VIDAS, THE DIRECTOR of United With Youth, was looking for a way to get youth and adults on board with asset building. He decided to take his concern to the experts—teenagers.

Working closely with a group of students selected from several local school districts, Vidas and other asset builders of the United Way and YMCA organized a Teen Symposium. This all-day conference brought more than 150 young people together to learn how they could serve as advocates for positive change. "When young people understand the developmental assets framework, they become empowered and talk with confidence about the changes they'd like to see in the community," says Vidas.

The three primary goals of this project were

to inform youth participants about the developmental assets, to review their community's results from the *Search Institute Profiles of Student Life: Attitudes and Behaviors* survey, and to call young people to action. Forty youth leaders teamed up with adults to facilitate group discussions and encourage their peers.

Since the event, Vidas has created a database of several hundred young people in the community who are equipped with asset-building knowledge and looking for opportunities to make a positive difference. "Empowering youth to make decisions is a good thing," says Vidas. "Adults need to be willing to give up some of that power."

# PASS IT ON **AT SCHOOL!**

TIPS FOR USING **Activity Handout 5**

## HOW TO USE THIS HANDOUT

This activity will take some time to develop in your school community. Paul Vidas offers the following tips for getting started:

- Focus on students. "Adults, though very active in planning, played limited roles," says Vidas.

- Involve students from different communities. "So often we gather our students to compete instead of working together," he says. "Here, almost 400 young people discussed what was valuable to themselves and their communities. They felt motivated and eager to begin."

- Let the developmental assets model guide your efforts. Vidas says that the research and positive focus will ring true to young people and adults.

- Try a "talk show" format to present information. Organizers arranged for the event to be taped, and at one point in the daylong activity, students participated in a "television show" that focused on asset building and giving young people meaningful roles.

- Small group discussion and large group reporting help clarify thinking.

- Training is a very valuable resource. A week before the activity, all of the youth and adult facilitators were taught how to use various equipment, and take notes, and they were given an overview of the developmental assets framework.

- Young people are up to the challenge. "The individuals on the advisory group picked up major tasks, including creating a database for the registrants, setting up the facilitator's training, and designing various forms," says Vidas.

- Keep your presentation on schedule.

Use the following handout to recruit young people who might be willing to help develop a student-led conference. Another helpful tip: If your school doesn't have the time or resources to develop such an activity, you might consider inviting individual classrooms to have a student-led discussion about various issues that concern them and turning those ideas over to the student council.

## NOTES:

For more ideas, see *An Asset Builder's Guide to Youth Leadership* and *You Have to Live It* (video), available from Search Institute. In addition, *Change of Heart: A Student and Staff Asset-Building Retreat* is a two-day event that helps a selected group of students, teachers, administrators, and support staff consider how to improve their school environment. All participants are selected through a schoolwide survey administered by the school prior to the retreat. For more information about this Search Institute training, visit our Web site: www.search-institute.org/training

# STUDENT SYMPOSIUM QUESTIONNAIRE

Do you think our school could be a better place for students? Do you wish that teachers and other staff members would give you a chance to voice your opinion about what would make school a more supportive place for you and your peers? We're organizing a schoolwide conference that focuses on these and other important issues. If you are interested, fill out this form and return it to

_____. **Thanks!**

Name (optional) _____

Homeroom _____

What are the top three things that you think could be improved about our school?

1. _____

2. _____

3. _____

# PASS IT ON **AT SCHOOL!**

**Activity Handout 5**

How would you change the three things that you mentioned on the other side?

1. _____

2. _____

3. _____


Why do you think this is so important?




Is there anything else you think we should know?

# PEER TUTORING

---

**KEY USER/S**
School staff, general student population

**ASSET CATEGORY**
Support, Boundaries and Expectations,
Commitment to Learning

**ASSETS ADDRESSED**
#5, Caring School Climate
#15, Positive Peer Influence
#21, Achievement Motivation
#22, School Engagement
#24, Bonding to School

---

## KEEP THIS IN MIND

Building the assets that are tied to academic success can and should include a focus on supporting positive peer influence. Many students, high-achievers and otherwise, can be taught to be peer tutors in areas that interest them. In some instances, "average" students are better candidates because they are more likely to understand how a student struggling with a particular subject feels. Not only can teaching others quickly turn into a valuable way to build the self-esteem of peer tutors, but these experiences can also provide a source of support, connection to the school, and bonding for students who choose to participate.

## HOW TO USE THIS HANDOUT

The following handout can be used as an application to become a peer tutor. Once you've identified youth who would like to participate as tutors, instruction and orientation will likely be necessary for tutors (and the students being tutored) to be successful. An activity such as this will also require the help of other staff members and can also potentially include members of the surrounding community.

Consider this:

## A Peer Tutoring Story

Eric is an average student who has been tutored in the past. He is very interested in computer games and has developed good keyboarding skills in the process of using computer gaming software. Eric is asked to tutor a younger student who has poor keyboarding skills and does not have a computer at home to practice on. Several times per week, during the 30-minute tutoring session, Eric meets his student in the computer lab. During the first session, Eric learns that his student likes math. With the help of the computer lab teacher, Eric finds and loads a simple and fun math software program and shows his student how to use that program over the course of successive tutoring sessions. Eric rewards his student at the end of each session with words of encouragement and small treats like stickers or bookmarks. He gets to know his student well enough to figure out what he or she would like as a reward for doing a good job at the end of the school year. What makes Eric successful? How can peer tutoring improve the way students look at themselves and each other?

# PEER TUTORING

## PEER TUTORING APPLICATION

Is there a subject that you know you're really good in? Do you find yourself offering your time to help your friends with their homework? Would you like helping younger students with their assignments? You might be a perfect peer tutor! Fill out this application. If you need more information see

_____.

(REMEMBER! PEER TUTORING IS A GREAT ACTIVITY TO INCLUDE ON WORK OR COLLEGE APPLICATIONS.)

Name _____ Adviser/Homeroom _____

I think I would make a good peer tutor because:
(EXAMPLES: I AM A GOOD LISTENER, I'VE TUTORED BEFORE, AND I LIKE HELPING PEOPLE LEARN.)

This is what I'm good at:

# PASS IT ON **AT SCHOOL!** ——————————
## Activity Handout 6

This is what I'd like to teach other students:

These are some ideas about how I will teach it:

1. _____

2. _____

3. _____

This is what I will do during the first tutoring session:

This is how I will reward student progress. (Ideas may include saying something positive, using stamps, or handing out homemade bookmarks or certificates. You don't have to spend any money to be a great tutor!)

I think this activity will make our school a better place because:

# RANDOM ACTS OF KINDNESS

---

**KEY USER/S**
School community, general student population

**ASSET CATEGORY**
Boundaries and Expectations

**ASSETS ADDRESSED**
#15, Positive Peer Influence

---

## KEEP THIS IN MIND

Help students increase their positive peer influence within the school by encouraging each student to take personal responsibility for building strong, positive peer relationships—one act at a time, one day at a time. This can be accomplished through simple acts of kindness. When students intentionally look for ways to help, the whole climate of the school can change for the better. The benefits can be individual or span the entire school community.

## HOW TO USE THIS HANDOUT

Challenge students to become a positive influence in the lives of their peers. Ask them to do one positive thing each day for someone else. This challenge can be given in an advisory or homeroom class, or it can be organized on a class or schoolwide level. Ask students to write down one reason why doing something positive for others is a good idea (e.g., everyone needs support, it can make a person feel more

valued, it makes the "giver" feel good about her/himself). Assign students a specific date for turning in the journal entries.

If you plan to share these "acts" with others, be sure to give students the option of participating in this exercise. Here are some possible options for using journal entries:

- Post the reasons on a bulletin board or around the room. Then ask students to use the handout to keep an anonymous journal about what they do, how the other person reacts, and how the student feels.

- Read an entry a day to the students at the start of homeroom or class, publish all the entries in a small book, or ask the principal to read several entries to open and close each school assembly.

- Try a schoolwide activity and post the ideas along the hallways of the school or in the front office.

## NOTES:

# RANDOM ACTS OF KINDNESS

## (JOURNAL NOTES)

Use this worksheet to record and reflect on the good things that you did for someone else.

This was the problem or situation:

This is what I did:

This is how the other person reacted:

This is how I felt:

This was the problem or situation:

This is what I did:

This is how the other person reacted:

This is how I felt:

# PASS IT ON **AT SCHOOL!** ———————————

**Activity Handout 7**

This was the problem or situation:

This is what I did:

This is how the other person reacted:

This is how I felt:

This was the problem or situation:

This is what I did:

This is how the other person reacted:

This is how I felt:

**JOURNAL ENTRIES ARE DUE** _____

# POWER ROLE MODELING

## KEEP THIS IN MIND

Many young people are unaware of the power
they have to influence others. As a result, some
may be less likely to consider what kind of
role model they might be for their peers. A
little awareness raising may be in order to help
students make more conscious choices about
what effect they want to have on those around
them. Leader, friend, negotiator, comedian—
young people can console, direct, calm, influence, or lighten the day through humor. Students
who make conscious choices about what they
want to model are students who believe they have
something meaningful to contribute—they feel
that what they do and who they are really matters.

## HOW TO USE THIS HANDOUT

The following handout includes five role-playing
scenarios that will help students better understand how important their words and
actions are in the school community. Student
retreats, homeroom, after-school programs, well-
ness classes, or even social studies classes are
great places to try this activity. Here's what you
can say to students:

"You may not always think so, but what you do,
say, and think matters. Why? Because your actions
(or lack of them) can affect another person either
positively or negatively. This is something that we
need to be especially aware of in our school. Let's
consider and discuss the following questions:

- Do you have the power to influence those
  around you? Why or why not?

- How much time do you spend criticizing
  other people? Why do you do it?

- What kind of role model do you want to be?"

Ask students to pair up with another person (or
form a team of four or five people) and role-play
one of the situations described on the handout.
Use one of the following ideas to make role playing more interactive and interesting for students:

- Set up a court situation or a for/against de-
  bate in which one student must convince the
  "jury" or the "judges" (the rest of the class)
  to believe a certain story or viewpoint, and
  another student must argue the opposing
  side. After the class reaches the "decision,"
  ask class members to tell each student what
  they did that influenced the final verdict.

- Assign roles to four students: leader-friend-negotiator-comedian or positive-negative-uninvolved-indecisive. Roles for younger students might be nice-mean-don't care, or ask them to react in a single way, such as smile-frown-laugh-ignore. Pose a situation and let them loose to play their assigned roles. Talk about what happened and ask them: Who had the most positive influence and why?

- Ask the students to set up their own roles and situations.

- Ask students to act out assigned roles through music. For example, assign various roles one day, ask students to choose music that reflects their role, and invite them to bring that music to play the next day in class. This activity allows you to assign many roles, one for each class member.

- Pose a situation, assign each class member a role, and ask them to come back in a few days with some way of playing that role, through acting, art, photography, music, dance, mime, creative writing—whatever helps them play the role and influence the situation.

## Additional Ways to Make Role Playing More Effective:

- **Make it relevant.** Role playing shouldn't focus on irrelevant situations that students can't understand or identify with.
- **Practice what you teach.** Take some time to rehearse what you might say to students in front of a colleague or other adult before you attempt to teach this new skill to students.
- **Don't embarrass students.** Role playing can be potentially embarrassing for students. Make the activity as simple as possible in the beginning and increase the degree of difficulty as the students' confidence increases.
- **Provide effective feedback.** Feedback can be done immediately after role playing. Ask students to make sure that all feedback is positive and to point out the strengths of their various styles.

*Contributed by Clay Roberts, Search Institute trainer and consultant for Vision Training Associates.*

# POWER ROLE MODELING

Are you a good role model? How would you act in the following five situations? What might the impact on the situation be if you act a certain way?

1. One student is bullying (verbally or physically) in an unsupervised area of the school. No adults are around to intervene.

2. A student is bragging in the cafeteria that he's going to bring a gun to school.

3. A student drops a tray in the cafeteria.

4. A substitute teacher has lost control of a class because a few students talk out loud and ignore the teacher.

5. A student at the board in math class hasn't yet been able to work out the problems correctly.

# ON THE SAME PAGE

**KEY USER/S**
Administrators, student
organizations, teachers

**ASSET CATEGORY**
Commitment to Learning

**ASSETS ADDRESSED**
#22, School Engagement
#25, Reading for Pleasure

**NOTES:**

## KEEP THIS IN MIND

Research tells us that students who read for
pleasure at least three hours a week have a
better chance of being successful in the classroom. However, being engaged in a good book
is often a distant second choice behind getting
engrossed in electronic activities such as computers, video games, and television. Students (and
parents) can be encouraged to read for pleasure
through a schoolwide reading activity or contest.

## HOW TO USE THIS HANDOUT

The handout can help you organize a schoolwide reading-for-pleasure program. Engage students to create a list of books to be read for fun
each month throughout the school year. Use the
handout as a checklist or to-do list that will help
you plan, organize, and publicize the event and
reward readers.

For more information on how to integrate developmental assets into your school curriculum, see *Powerful Teaching: Developmental Assets in Curriculum and Instruction*, available from Search Institute. Visit our Web site: www.search-institute.org.

# ON THE SAME PAGE

## TO-DO/CHECKLIST FOR CREATING A SCHOOLWIDE "READING-FOR-PLEASURE" PROGRAM

❏ Recruit a volunteer organizing committee that includes interested students, teachers, school staff, and parents or guardians. Don't forget the custodians, office and food service workers, school bus drivers, and coaches.

❏ Ask the group to find a way to poll everyone in the school about books they would like to recommend.

❏ Select a book for each month and publicize it everywhere. Involve the school and community librarians to make sure enough copies are available for those who don't wish to buy the books or can't afford them.

❏ Consider tying the reading-for-pleasure program to an in-school buddy or tutoring program. Student tutors can help their assigned students to read the book of the month.

❏ Create a forum for discussion at the end of each month or reading period. This could be a gathering during the day or evening (so parents and community members can participate), presentations, or an on-line chat room discussion set up on the school Web site.

❏ Track reading progress on a public bulletin board. Make small circles or book cutouts available on which readers can write their name and the name of each book they've read. When all of these are pinned to a large bulletin board located in a public area of the school, more students, staff, and parents will want to "join up."

❏ Ask the committee to think of ways to advertise the event, the readers, and the discussions in school newsletters and on the Web site, at parent and staff meetings, and even in community newspapers.

❏ Find ways for people to share their pleasure! Create special school newspaper, Web site, or bulletin board space for reader reviews.

❏ Create awards that are given along the way and at the end of the school year or end of the reading program. Reward those who have read all the books and those who have made presentations or done other things to spur discussion. Reward special education and other students with specific challenges for reading some of the books or for finding ways to participate in the reading project.

# SCHOOLWIDE ASSET-BUILDING PROJECT (TWO-PART HANDOUT)

**KEY USER/S**
School leaders (students and adults), community partners

**ASSET CATEGORY**
All

**ASSETS ADDRESSED**
All

## KEEP THIS IN MIND

One way for schools to approach developing a schoolwide asset-building project is to introduce everyone who interacts within the school environment to the overall philosophy, familiarize them with all 40 assets, and then select a few assets for yearlong focus. Once the school community at large is immersed in the asset-building model and has absorbed the philosophy and language of building assets among students, choosing key assets can be highly effective. The assets selected for yearlong emphasis can be identified and selected based on the input of each segment of the school community:  each class of students, faculty, administrators, coaches, school board members, members of the parent-teacher organization, parents or guardians, and volunteers.

## HOW TO USE THESE HANDOUTS

The following handouts serve as an easy way to raise awareness, get the school community on board with your efforts to build assets, and survey students and adults about their picks for the top three assets that they would like to focus on during the school year. Distribute the handouts during presentations and meetings and feel free to use videos, books, and other materials to help others better understand the concept.

Here are some things to consider before you begin:

- Identify the key groups who interact within the school community.

- Orient each group to fostering positive student growth through the 40 developmental assets. Orientation and midyear retreats are good settings in which to present faculty with a cohesive sense of the asset model. Parents, school board members, and volunteers can be invited to a special evening for presentation of the asset model. Students can be approached during advisories or in special assemblies.

- Provide opportunities to explore and support the asset themes in faculty meetings, parent-teacher conferences, parent meetings, student assemblies, student council meetings, and classrooms and on closed-circuit television.

# PASS IT ON **AT SCHOOL!**
## TIPS FOR USING **Activity Handout 10**

- At the end of the school year, survey students and staff to assess their knowledge of the selected assets and the impact that knowledge and accompanying handouts had on each individual.

- The following school year, publicize the survey results and engage the school community once again in selecting specific assets for year-long attention. Help the larger school community become more familiar with the asset-building philosophy by keeping messages consistent and redundant for new students and families and for the existing student body.

**NOTES:**

# SCHOOLWIDE ASSET-BUILDING PROJECT (TWO-PART HANDOUT)

## PART 1: A SURVEY FOR STUDENTS AND ADULTS

Help make our school a better place for *everyone!*

All of us have the potential to positively influence the lives of the people around us. Let's focus on the assets that our school can start intentionally building. Below is a list of the developmental assets. Place a check next to the three assets that you think should be an important priority in our school.

## EXTERNAL ASSETS

### SUPPORT

___ 1. **Family support**—Family life provides high levels of love and support.

___ 2. **Positive family communication**—Young person and her or his parent(s) communicate positively, and young person is willing to seek advice and counsel from parent(s).

___ 3. **Other adult relationships**—Young person receives support from three or more nonparent adults.

___ 4. **Caring neighborhood**—Young person experiences caring neighbors.

___ 5. **Caring school climate**—School provides a caring, encouraging environment.

___ 6. **Parent involvement in schooling**—Parent(s) are actively involved in helping the young person succeed in school.

## EMPOWERMENT

___ 7. **Community values youth**—Young person perceives that adults in the community value youth.

___ 8. **Youth as resources**—Young people are given useful roles in the community.

___ 9. **Service to others**—Young person serves in the community one hour or more per week.

___ 10. **Safety**—Young person feels safe at home, at school, and in the neighborhood.

## BOUNDARIES AND EXPECTATIONS

___ 11. **Family boundaries**—Family has clear rules and consequences and monitors the young person's whereabouts.

___ 12. **School boundaries**—School provides clear rules and consequences.

___ 13. **Neighborhood boundaries**—Neighbors take responsibility for monitoring young people's behavior.

___ 14. **Adult role models**—Parent(s) and other adults model positive, responsible behavior.

___ 15. **Positive peer influence**—Young person's best friends model responsible behavior.

___ 16. **High expectations**—Both parent(s) and teachers encourage the young person to do well.

# PASS IT ON **AT SCHOOL!**
## Activity Handout 10: PART 1

## CONSTRUCTIVE USE OF TIME

___ 17. **Creative activities**—Young person spends three or more hours per week in lessons or practice in music, theater, or other arts.

___ 18. **Youth programs**—Young person spends three or more hours per week in sports, clubs, or organizations at school and/or in the community.

___ 19. **Religious community**—Young person spends one or more hours per week in activities in a religious institution.

___ 20. **Time at home**—Young person is out with friends "with nothing special to do" two or fewer nights per week.

# INTERNAL ASSETS

## COMMITMENT TO LEARNING

___ 21. **Achievement motivation**—Young person is motivated to do well in school.

___ 22. **School engagement**—Young person is actively engaged in learning.

___ 23. **Homework**—Young person reports doing at least one hour of homework every school day.

___ 24. **Bonding to school**—Young person cares about her or his school.

___ 25. **Reading for pleasure**—Young person reads for pleasure three or more hours per week.

## POSITIVE VALUES

___ 26. **Caring**—Young person places high value on helping other people.

___ 27. **Equality and social justice**—Young person places high value on promoting equality and reducing hunger and poverty.

___ 28. **Integrity**—Young person acts on convictions and stands up for her or his beliefs.

___ 29. **Honesty**—Young person "tells the truth even when it is not easy."

___ 30. **Responsibility**—Young person accepts and takes personal responsibility.

___ 31. **Restraint**—Young person believes it is important not to be sexually active or to use alcohol or other drugs.

## SOCIAL COMPETENCIES

___ 32. **Planning and decision making**—Young person knows how to plan ahead and make choices.

___ 33. **Interpersonal competence**—Young person has empathy, sensitivity, and friendship skills.

___ 34. **Cultural competence**—Young person has knowledge of and comfort with people of different cultural/racial/ethnic backgrounds.

___ 35. **Resistance skills**—Young person can resist negative peer pressure and dangerous situations.

___ 36. **Peaceful conflict resolution**—Young person seeks to resolve conflict nonviolently.

## POSITIVE IDENTITY

___ 37. **Personal power**—Young person feels he or she has control over "things that happen to me."

___ 38. **Self-esteem**—Young person reports having a high self-esteem.

___ 39. **Sense of purpose**—Young person reports that "my life has a purpose."

___ 40. **Positive view of personal future**—Young person is optimistic about her or his personal future.

Thank you for caring about our school community!

**Please indicate here if you would like to help us build these assets at our school and return this form to:**

Name_____

Homeroom/Phone/Email

_____

# SCHOOLWIDE ASSET-BUILDING PROJECT (TWO-PART HANDOUT)

## PART 2: RESULTS OF THE SCHOOLWIDE ASSET-BUILDING PROJECT SURVEY

_____ People in our school community said that assets were a priority in the school, by completing the survey.

Here are the top three assets selected by survey participants:

1. _____

2. _____

3. _____

We're excited about building assets in our school community!

If you would like to participate in further discussions about this survey, developmental assets, and helping all students succeed, please write your name and contact information below and return this form to _____.

---

**YES!** I WANT TO HELP BUILD ASSETS IN OUR SCHOOL!

Name _____

Homeroom/Phone/Email _____

Additional Comments:

---

# CELEBRATE ACHIEVEMENTS

**KEY USER/S**
School staff, administrators

**ASSET CATEGORY**
Positive Identity

**ASSETS ADDRESSED**
#37, Personal Power
#38, Self-Esteem
#39, Sense of Purpose

## KEEP THIS IN MIND

When students do well, tell them about it! It's a great way to nurture a positive identity in students. This kind of recognition can be done either individually (one-on-one) or, even better, publicly. Schools can create reward programs that regularly celebrate student achievements. Not only is this a wonderful tradition to pass on for years to come, it's a great way to change the culture of a school by motivating students to work toward such an honor.

## HOW TO USE THIS HANDOUT

This handout contains ideas for student award programs and events. School staff can use this list as a starting point to generate ideas about the type of student achievement the school wants to acknowledge and how to do it. The program or event can take place annually or biannually (depending on your school) and can involve staff members, students, and parents.

## NOTES:

# CELEBRATE ACHIEVEMENTS

**Students deserve our recognition when they strive to be and do their best. The following is a short list of ideas for making every young person in our school community feel valuable. Please feel free to add (and share) your own ideas and give them to**

_____ .

- **AWARDS ASSEMBLY**
  _Here's one way to do it:_ Establish a tradition of having an all-school awards assembly once or twice a year. Create awards categories for achievement in each of the asset categories: support, empowerment, boundaries and expectations, constructive use of time, commitment to learning, positive values, social competencies, and positive identity.

- **EXTRACURRICULAR AWARDS**
  _Here's one way to do it:_ Put trophies, certificates, or other awards on public display in a trophy case used expressly for showing the latest extracurricular achievements. Use a bulletin board next to the case to list names of those involved and post photos of the events when available. Put captions on photos as a way to acknowledge individual students involved in the event. The key is to recognize the MVP _as well as_ the best musician, artist, or scientist so that students feel appreciated for their individual talents and gifts.

- **FROM THE PRINCIPAL'S DESK**
  _Here's one way to do it:_ Periodically distribute a short newsletter giving praise for student and

teacher achievements. Give it a title like "The Monthly Who's Who at XX High" or "Stars of the Month" or "XX Middle School's Best and Brightest of the Month."(Add another level of asset building by giving books as prizes.)

- **NONTRADITIONAL RECOGNITION/ "CAUGHT IN THE ACT"**
  _Here's one way to do it:_ Celebrate even the smallest achievement by regularly polling staff and students about the person who they believe has achieved the most over a certain period of time. Suggestions will vary—maybe a known bully was "caught" helping a younger student, or a "chatty" student sat through a class period without disturbing everyone else. Invite everyone to share her or his ideas.

- **A AND B HONOR ROLL**
  _Here's one way to do it:_ Post names on bulletin boards in a public area of the school building, announce names after each grading period over the intercom or at student assemblies, and publish names in the school newsletter.

**OTHER IDEAS:** _____

_____

_____

_____

_____

# ASSET ALL-STARS

**KEY USER/S**
Schoolwide initiative

**ASSET CATEGORY**
Support, Positive Identity

**ASSETS ADDRESSED**
#5, Caring School Climate
#38, Self-Esteem

## KEEP THIS IN MIND

One way to "grow" student asset leaders is to reward young people for their intentional (or unintentional) efforts to build assets. Find the all-stars, those students who are doing things that reinforce assets—whether or not they know that's what they're doing. Schools can develop systematic ways to identify asset builders and encourage them by publicly acknowledging what they're doing. This activity not only recognizes the good things that are happening every day, it also builds awareness about asset building among all the members of the school community.

## HOW TO USE THIS HANDOUT

This activity can happen on the schoolwide level or on the classroom level, depending on your school's available resources. If your school community already has a way to publicly recognize students for their successes, this idea might be incorporated into that program. Ask students to support this idea by identifying peers who should be considered for a quarterly (weekly or monthly) "Asset All-Star Award" in each of the asset categories. Use the feedback to identify students who deserve public recognition for their activities.

## NOTES:

# ASSET ALL-STARS

## NOMINATE AN ALL-STAR!

The Asset All-Star Awards assembly recognizes students who try to make school a better place for other students and staff. Help us find the students who deserve our appreciation. If you know someone in the school who you think deserves an award in any of the following categories, please write her or his name and give a brief description of what that person has done and why you think he or she deserves recognition. Thanks for your help!

Name of student I'd like to nominate:

_____

Description of nominee's activities:

_____

Why I think this person deserves recognition:

_____

## AWARD CATEGORY

*(Select the asset category that best describes what the nominee has done to make the school community better):*

❑ **Support**—Young people need to be surrounded by people who love, care for, appreciate, and accept them.

❑ **Empowerment**—Young people need to feel valued and valuable. This happens when youth feel safe and respected.

❑ **Boundaries and Expectations**—Young people need clear rules, consistent consequences for breaking rules, and encouragement to do their best.

❑ **Constructive Use of Time**—Young people need opportunities—outside of school—to learn and develop new skills and interests with other youth and adults.

❑ **Commitment to Learning**—Young people need a sense of the lasting importance of learning and a belief in their own abilities.

❑ **Positive Values**—Young people need to develop strong guiding values or principles to help them make healthy life choices.

❑ **Social Competencies**—Young people need the skills to interact effectively with others, to make difficult decisions, and to cope with new situations.

❑ **Positive Identity**—Young people need to believe in their own self-worth and to feel that they have control over the things that happen to them.

*Optional: It's okay to contact me for further information.*

Your name _____

Your homeroom/adviser

_____

# INTEGRATING ASSETS IN SCHOOLS

**KEY USER/S**
Administrators, student organizations, teachers

**ASSET CATEGORY**
All

**ASSETS ADDRESSED**
All

## KEEP THIS IN MIND

Schoolwide asset-building efforts can benefit from the support of everyone, particularly staff members and parents. Build awareness and interest by asking teachers, staff, administrators, and parents to brainstorm ideas for bringing the entire school community on board with the concept of asset building.

## HOW TO USE THIS HANDOUT

Use the handout to spur discussion at staff or parent meetings, planning sessions, and retreats. Encourage individuals to pair up or gather in small groups to brainstorm potential opportunities for asset building in the school. The tips in the handout serve as a guide for what the people who are a part of the school community can do to create a better place for all youth.

**NOTES:**

# INTEGRATING ASSETS IN SCHOOLS

| Ideas for integrating the developmental assets into schools | How our school can accomplish this |
|---|---|
| Always link asset building and asset attainment to student achievement. | |
| Actively seek the support of building and district-level administrators as well as student services personnel (social workers, counselors, prevention specialists). | |
| Make the connection between positive school climate, optimal learning environment, and the asset framework and philosophy. | |
| Expect lasting change to be the result of everyone becoming an asset builder. | |
| Develop a three-to-five-year strategic plan. (For example, in three years all of our paperwork on students will contain asset language.) | |
| Involve parents or guardians from the beginning. | |
| Involve students from the beginning (leadership, service—learning, meaningful participation in school, student panels about the importance of asset builders in their lives). | |

# PASS IT ON **AT SCHOOL!**
### Activity Handout 13

| Ideas for integrating the developmental assets into schools | How our school can accomplish this |
|---|---|
| Asset-pack existing programs and practices to get to the intentional level of asset building. | |
| Continually promote, support, and celebrate asset-building behaviors throughout the school community. | |
| Nurture asset champions and continually bring new ones along. | |
| Continually inform, teach, and guide students, staff, and parents about assets and asset building. | |

*Contributed by Christine Beyer, Search Institute trainer and consultant for Vision Training Associates.*

For more information about integrating the developmental assets framework into your school community, see "Ask a researcher: Are developmental assets related to school success?" Found in *Assets: The Magazine of Ideas for Healthy Communities and Healthy Youth,* Autumn 2002. Also see *Great Places to Learn: How Asset-Building Schools Help Students Succeed* by Neal Starkman, Peter C. Scales, and Clay Roberts. Both are available from Search Institute.

# SAFE SCHOOLS

**KEY USER/S**
Administrators, school staff, student
organizations

**ASSET CATEGORY**
Support, Empowerment, Positive
Values, Social Competencies

**ASSETS ADDRESSED**
#5, Caring School Climate
#10, Safety
#31, Restraint
#35, Resistance skills
#36, Peaceful Conflict Resolution

**NOTES:**

## KEEP THIS IN MIND

One important part of making students feel
comfortable in their school is addressing how to
make the environment safe. School communities
can accomplish this by bringing youth and adults
to the table to talk about building a safe place
where all students and staff are appreciated and
valued.

## HOW TO USE THIS HANDOUT

The following handout can be used to plan strategies that engage everyone in working to promote a safe school environment. Strategies like
these can help change the way students feel
about their school and can address many safety
issues, including violence, gang activity, alcohol
and other drug use, and bullying.

# SAFE SCHOOLS

## SAFE SCHOOL STRATEGY PLANNER FOR PROMOTING A SAFE SCHOOL ENVIRONMENT

| ASSET TO PROMOTE | STRATEGY | ACTION STEPS |
|---|---|---|
| #31, Restraint | Create a school culture in which high-risk behaviors such as smoking and alcohol and other drug use are not acceptable. | Provide supervised activities that fully engage students and make them feel important, respected, and needed. Teach them resistance skills. |
| #35, Resistance Skills | Help students resist negative peer pressure and dangerous situations. | Find opportunities to help students identify dangerous situations and think of ways to prevent them or handle them by making healthy choices. |
| #36, Peaceful Conflict Resolution | Promote peaceful and safe interactions. | All school staff model respectful interacting. Institute a conflict resolution program. Offer anger management programs for students and staff. |

# PASS IT ON **AT SCHOOL!**

## ADDITIONAL STRATEGIES FOR PROMOTING
## A CARING SCHOOL ENVIRONMENT

| ASSET TO PROMOTE | STRATEGY | ACTION STEPS |
|---|---|---|
| | | |
| | | |
| | | |

# PASS IT ON **AT SCHOOL!**
TIPS FOR USING **Activity Handout 15**

# MIX IT UP

> **KEY USER/S**
> School community
>
> **ASSET CATEGORY**
> Support, Positive Values, Social
> Competencies
>
> **ASSETS ADDRESSED**
> #5, Caring School Climate
> #27, Equality and Social Justice
> #34, Cultural Competence

## KEEP THIS IN MIND

An important asset in the social competencies area of the developmental assets framework is cultural competence. Young people need to build knowledge of and comfort with people of cultural, racial, and ethnic backgrounds different from their own. Typically, as in adult society, the tendency of many students is to stick to one group with which they most closely identify. Schools can encourage students and leadership groups within the school community to develop a yearlong campaign that encourages cultural competence among all students.

## HOW TO USE THIS HANDOUT

The first step in accomplishing this activity is to identify the young people who can help develop a schoolwide campaign. Staff and students can identify all the student groups that exist within the school, both curricular and extracurricular (sports teams, clubs, etc.). Ask students, student advisers, coaches, and other staff to provide the name of key students in each group. Next, invite these students to a meeting to brainstorm ideas to help young people appreciate and celebrate the diversity of your school community. Have a pizza party (or provide other snacks), open up the topic, and then sit back and listen. Help the group pull ideas together into a few clearly defined action steps with a timetable and plan for implementing the ideas. Use the handout as a discussion starter, to help students think of things that might work in their school.

## NOTES:

# MIX IT UP

## DISCUSSION STARTER

Ideas for ways to mix it up and get comfortable outside your group

1. **Tell it, Teach it.** Students share something that reflects their cultural, racial, or ethnic background. They then teach that activity, craft, or skill to another student or small group of students. These students master the activity or skill and then demonstrate it for a larger school assembly or event.

2. **Families, too.** Ask students to recruit parents or guardians, grandparents, or other adult relatives or friends to come to the school to share some aspect of their heritage. This can be done in individual classrooms, during a separate Heritage Day, or periodically during school assemblies.

3. **Pick a number.** Have students coordinate one day each week when students coming into the cafeteria pick a number from a hat. The numbers coincide with numbers placed on cafeteria seats. The students must sit at the numbered places rather than at their usual tables. Students who participate might be rewarded with a special treat (e.g., brownies, cookies, or ice cream) for dessert.

4. **Does our school appreciate diversity?** Ask students to consider the question and write about their experiences. Post them around the school anonymously.

5. **Senior-freshman buddy project.** Assign incoming freshmen to a member of the senior class and encourage positive interaction, which could include a pizza party, pep rally, or mid-semester mixer.

6. **Service beyond.** Is there a senior citizen community or preschool near the school? Organize a service project at one of these locations.

7. **Celebration potluck.** Host a special potluck that invites students (or even families) to bring foods that reflect their cultural and ethnic heritage.

8.

9.

10.

# YOUR VOICE IS IMPORTANT!

**KEY USER/S**
School community

**ASSET CATEGORY**
Empowerment, Positive Values,
Social Competencies

**ASSETS ADDRESSED**
#9, Service to Others
#27, Equality and Social Justice
#32, Planning and Decision Making
#33, Interpersonal Competence

## KEEP THIS IN MIND

Help young people find their prosocial voices!
Empathy is a tremendous asset for students of
all ages (as well as adults) to have. To develop
empathy, students need role models and they
must be challenged to "walk a mile in another's
shoes." Schools can motivate students to care
about something, to take on a cause, and find
ways to rally attention and help for that cause.
The result? Confident, successful students who
have found their voices and believe they are important members of the school community with
the power to change things for the better. School
boards, administrators, principals, teachers, and
others within the school community can become
the moving force for creating ways to help students find their prosocial voices.

## HOW TO USE THIS HANDOUT

The handout can be copied and distributed
throughout the school as a way to gather ideas
from youth and adults about how the school can
help the community improve for the better. Follow-up will be especially important after students
have completed the forms. This may include
pulling together a small group of interested students after school, making a formal presentation
to all students, or asking homeroom teachers
to lead follow-up discussions with students. You
might even ask a math class to compile the results and come up with a report about what students have written.

## NOTE

# YOUR VOICE IS IMPORTANT!

Many problems and issues need attention, and many individuals, groups, and organizations could use a helping hand. As a school, we're looking for ways to involve our entire school community in helping others in our neighborhood, country, and world. We'd like your ideas about how we can and should get involved. Tell us how you think our school can make a difference.

1. This is an issue or problem I think needs to be addressed: _____

   _____

2. This is why I think it should be addressed: _____

   _____

3. I think our school can help by: _____

   _____

4. These are some other details that might help the school organize our students and staff to help:

   _____

I am willing to work on this idea:          Yes          No

My contact information *(optional):*

Name _____

Student _____ School staff member ___ Parent/Guardian ___

Adviser/Homeroom _____

PASS IT ON **AT SCHOOL!** ————————
TIPS FOR USING **Activity Handout 17**

# STUDENT ASSET TRAINERS

**KEY USER/S**
Schoolwide initiatives, youth
involvement/leadership

**ASSET CATEGORY**
Empowerment, Positive Values,
Positive Identity

**ASSETS ADDRESSED**
#8, Youth as Resources
#26, Caring
#39, Sense of Purpose

## KEEP THIS IN MIND

Tap into the power students have to influence
and lead others! Students can be taught about
the developmental assets and how to share these
messages with others. In some instances, young
people will be far more able than adults to per-
suade other youth and adults to build assets in
the community.

## HOW TO USE THIS HANDOUT

The handout will help schools teach students
to build awareness about asset building among
other students, parents, and school staff. It can
be used as a guide for students to follow during
presentations/meetings to help them touch on
the key ideas they need to convey about asset
building.

**NOTES:**

# STUDENT ASSET TRAINERS

When you first hear about them, the developmental assets may not seem like the easiest concept to understand. Here are some basic facts that you can share with young people and adults in your school and community:

## ASSET-BUILDING IDEAS

**1. What are assets?**

The assets are 40 important factors young people need for healthy growth and development.

**2. How were the assets developed?**

Search Institute, a nonprofit, independent research organization based in Minneapolis, Minnesota, wanted to know the answers to some questions:

- Why do some young people grow up with ease, while others struggle?
- Why do some young people get involved in dangerous activities, while others spend their time contributing to society?
- Why do some youth "beat the odds" in difficult situations, while others get trapped?

They identified 40 concrete, positive experiences and qualities—called developmental assets—that have a big influence on young people's lives and choices.

**3. Why are the assets important to learn about?**

Research shows that the 40 developmental assets help young people make wise decisions, choose positive paths, and grow up competent, caring, and responsible. Most young people experience too few of the assets: on average, surveyed youth reported experiencing just 19 of the 40 assets.

**4. Who can help young people build assets?**

Everyone! A child, teenager, single adult, parent, grandparent—anyone can build assets.

**5. What are the specific assets?**

**EXTERNAL ASSETS**

The first 20 developmental assets focus on positive experiences that young people receive from the people and institutions in their lives. Four categories of external assets are included in the framework:

- **Support**—Young people need to experience support, care, and love from their families, neighbors, and many others. They need organizations and institutions that provide positive, supportive environments.
- **Empowerment**—Young people need to be valued by their community and have opportunities to contribute to others. For this to occur, they must be safe and feel secure.
- **Boundaries and expectations**—Young people need to know what is expected of them and whether activities and behaviors are "in bounds" or "out of bounds."

- **Constructive use of time**—Young people need constructive, enriching opportunities for growth through creative activities, youth programs, congregational involvement, and quality time at home.

### INTERNAL ASSETS:

The internal assets guide choices, create a sense of purpose, and encourage wise, responsible, and compassionate judgments. Four categories of internal assets are included in the framework:

- **Commitment to learning**—Young people need to develop a lifelong commitment to education and learning.
- **Positive values**—Youth need to develop strong values that guide their choices.
- **Social competencies**—Young people need skills and competencies that equip them to make positive choices, to build relationships, and to succeed in life.
- **Positive identity**—Young people need a strong sense of their own power, purpose, worth, and promise.

### 6. How can you become an asset builder?

Many things you personally do, or could do, every day make a big difference. Here are eight ways you can build developmental assets—one for each category of assets. (Many of these ideas are geared toward adults, but if you're a young person, you can do the same things for your friends and younger children whom you know.)

- *Support* young people with your caring and attention.
- *Empower* them to use their abilities to help others.
- Set reasonable *boundaries and* have high *expectations.*
- Help them find activities that make *constructive use of* their *time.*
- Spark their *commitment to learning.*

- Guide them toward a life based on *positive values.*
- Help them develop *social competencies* and life skills.
- Celebrate their uniqueness and affirm their *positive identity.*

# INVISIBLE MENTORS

## KEEP THIS IN MIND

Invisible mentoring can serve as a wonderful, intentional way to build assets within the school community. Teachers can become mentors for students by identifying young people who can benefit from a positive relationship with a caring adult outside of their family. Invite staff members to mentor a student without her or him knowing about it.

The mentor should be encouraged to find opportunities to build a relationship through gradual, yet consistent, positive interaction. Such personal connections can begin with a quick and friendly chat in the hallway or lunchroom and can eventually lead to lasting relationships students and staff can depend on.

This technique can also be successful when the students serve as mentors to teachers. Not only does it give students a sense of purpose within the school community, it also encourages young people to connect with adults in a way that is healthy and fun.

## HOW TO ORGANIZE INVISIBLE MENTORS

Make a list of those to be mentored, whether students, teachers, or other school staff. Ask the potential mentors to choose the name of someone they don't know well. This is the person to be mentored "invisibly" throughout the school year. Place a mark by the names as they are selected and ask for volunteers to take on any names not chosen. Other options include simply selecting names from a box, or asking the students or teachers to suggest a way to choose names.

## HOW TO USE THIS HANDOUT

Use the following handout to organize either a teacher-to-student or student-to-teacher mentoring project.

## NOTES:

18

# INVISIBLE MENTORS

*Thank you for helping us create a more connected and caring school community! As an invisible mentor, you will have the opportunity to share your gifts and talents with someone else in the school. Remember, in order for this to be successful, it's important that you keep your identity a secret.*

**Think about the following questions:**

What are my top three reasons for deciding to be a mentor?

1. _____

2. _____

3. _____

What are the things I hope to accomplish when this project ends?

1. _____

2. _____

3. _____

**Getting Started**

Not sure how to begin? Here are some simple ideas for getting started. (Feel free to write your ideas in the space provided.)

- Think of ways to reach out to students and staff members who don't have a strong relationship with the school and find ways to secretly give them attention.
- Find ways to let the person you're mentoring know that her or his ideas and opinions are valuable.
- Leave a note saying how much you appreciate your assigned adult or student on her or his desk or locker.
- Be the first to say "hi" in the hallway, lunchroom, or classroom.
- Encourage your peers to show respect for all staff members and students.

**My ideas . . .**

# CELEBRATE DIVERSITY EVERY DAY

**KEY USER/S**
School community

**ASSET CATEGORY**
Empowerment, Constructive Use of Time, Positive Values, Social Competencies

**ASSETS ADDRESSED**
#8, Youth as Resources
#17, Creative Activities
#27, Equality and Social Justice
#34, Cultural Competence

## KEEP THIS IN MIND

Efforts to experience and appreciate people of diverse backgrounds, languages, and regions of the world are so valuable to the development of young people that it should be a daily activity or focus. Unfortunately, diversity is often only a topic of the day or focus of a single month. Schools can create a number of activities that encourage students as well as teachers and school staff to immerse themselves in diversity each day. This includes using instructional strategies such as cooperative learning and differentiation of curriculum and instruction to celebrate differences and build connections.

## HOW TO USE THIS HANDOUT

Help students and school staff celebrate diversity all year long by seeking out activities that require daily interaction, activity, or focus. The following handout is meant to generate ideas for yearlong diversity experiences. It can be used to solicit ideas *by* anyone *with* any one group within the school. Teachers can sit down with students and ask them to come up with ideas. Students can ask teachers or other students. Principals can ask teachers, school staff, students, the school board, and so forth.

## NOTES:

# CELEBRATE DIVERSITY EVERY DAY

Here are some ideas for encouraging and appreciating diversity every day of the year. What suggestions do you have that might be especially appropriate for our school?

- Around-the-World Email Trail: Set up a letter-writing or email writing project that involves anyone in the school who wishes to participate. Students can email other students, or teachers can email other teachers in the United States or around the world. Post a large map in the classroom, cafeteria, or staff lounge and use colorful pushpins to mark each location where a school student or staff member is connected with someone. A coordinating person or group can gather comments from the emailers or letter writers to assemble into a monthly newsletter to let the larger school community know more about these exchanges and perhaps encourage others to join in.

- Participation in language clubs can be encouraged with an all-school goal of having everyone in the school—teachers, other school staff, and students—participate. Open the language clubs to those who don't have the time to learn the language in depth, but who want to know more about the culture of the countries where that language is spoken.

- Build ties with a local senior citizen residence or community. Create one-on-one pairings as well as ways for groups to interact. Then share what they are learning about each other.

- Go beyond diversity activities that are often arranged for a particular month or in honor of a few well-known multicultural leaders. Look for ways to study diversity issues and history throughout the school year and across the curriculum (for example, reading biographies of women and men who were first to achieve something).

- Set up a project that involves students identifying other young people who are making a positive difference in the world.

- Encourage students or anyone in the school to get interested in a cause. Organizers (students or adults) can identify the cause, find ways to help others understand the issues involved, and take action steps to make a difference.

- Find out the demographics of your school now and 20 years ago. How have things changed?

# SHARE YOUR SPIRIT

**KEY USER/S**
Students, staff members

**ASSET CATEGORY**
Support, Empowerment,
Constructive Use of Time,
Social Competencies

**ASSETS ADDRESSED**
#5, Caring School Climate
#7, Community Values Youth
#17, Creative Activities
#34, Cultural Competence

**NOTES:**

## KEEP THIS IN MIND

Invite everyone in your school community to
share what makes them unique. Ask students and
staff members to tell their individual stories anonymously and post them in a prominent place
in the school for everyone to read and enjoy.
This activity can bring students and staff closer
together and serve as a vivid example of your
school's appreciation and respect for diversity.

## HOW TO USE THIS HANDOUT

Encourage students and staff to fill out the
following handout, reminding them that their
thoughts will be displayed for others to read
and reflect on throughout the school or in the
classroom.

# SHARE YOUR SPIRIT

**WHAT MAKES YOU UNIQUE?** Think about how you would complete the following sentences. Feel free to write your responses or draw a picture in the space provided.

I would use these words to describe me *(circle ones you feel apply)*:

| | | | |
|---|---|---|---|
| **Funny** | **Silly** | **Smart** | **Other words** |
| **Serious** | **Shy** | **Caring** | _____ |
| **Creative** | **Quiet** | **Clever** | _____ |
| **Outgoing** | **Strong** | **Fun** | _____ |

One thing that I really like about our school is . . .

If there was one thing I could change to make my school a better place, it would be . . .

I was born in . . . (city, state, country)

I live with . . .

One thing people don't know about me is . . .

I say this because . . .

# BATHROOM CENTRAL

---

**KEY USER/S**
School staff

**ASSET CATEGORY**
Support, Commitment to
Learning, Positive Values

**ASSETS ADDRESSED**
#5, Caring School Climate
#24, Bonding to School
#30, Responsibility

---

## KEEP THIS IN MIND

For many students, the bathroom is a quick and easy way to "escape" the pressures of a hectic school day. School bathrooms serve many purposes besides the obvious one. A bathroom can be a gathering place, a place to get some privacy or quiet time, or a place to hang out and be you. In many ways it's a place for free association. Capture the need for students to express themselves and channel that output into a positive outlet.

## HOW TO USE THIS HANDOUT

Use the tips list to create ways to channel the time students spend in bathrooms and the needs that these particular gathering places serve. Post copies of the survey in bathrooms to encourage students to improve their school environment.

## TIPS FOR IMPROVING BATHROOM "DECOR"

- Put a large sheet of blank paper on a bathroom wall along with some markers. Invite students to write or draw on it. Encourage students to keep their messages positive.

- Put posters with asset-building phrases or affirmations on the walls, or inside each stall.

- Post a volunteer sign-up list for students to take responsibility to help keep the bathrooms clean by picking up each time they use them.

- Post a list asking for suggestions to improve the look of the bathroom and ask for volunteers who are willing to do the work.

- Assemble a small book of affirmations for young people, make multiple copies, and attach them inside bathroom stalls.

- Place a list of student resources inside each stall, including help for issues related to abuse, sexuality, alcohol and other drug use, eating disorders, or other problems students might experience.

- Post information that challenges stereotypical ideas about beauty and body image.

# BATHROOM CENTRAL

For some students, this bathroom is a place to "escape" the pressures of a hectic school day. It's part of the school environment and part of your daily life. If you want to make it a more interesting place, please take time to fill out this survey and put it in the survey box in the main office.

## WHAT DO YOU THINK ABOUT THE APPEARANCE OF THIS BATHROOM?

_____

## WHAT'S BAD ABOUT IT?

_____

## WHAT'S GOOD ABOUT IT?

_____

## WHAT WOULD YOU DO TO CHANGE HOW IT LOOKS? PLEASE BE SPECIFIC.

_____

_____

_____

## IF YOU COULD PAINT IT A COLOR OR TWO, WHAT COLORS WOULD YOU USE?

_____

_____

# PASS IT ON **AT SCHOOL!**
**Activity Handout 21**

## IF YOU COULD **ADD A MURAL** HERE, WHAT IMAGES WOULD YOU LIKE TO SEE?
(SCHOOL MASCOT, ETC.)

_____

_____

## WHAT **OTHER CHANGES** WOULD YOU LIKE TO SEE MADE?

_____

_____

## IF THE SCHOOL NEEDED SOME **HELP** REDOING THE BATHROOMS, WOULD YOU VOLUNTEER? HOW CAN YOU HELP OUT?

_____

_____

## WHAT ARE **YOUR IDEAS** FOR KEEPING THE BATHROOM CLEAN?

_____

_____

I would like to be contacted about my ideas: **YES**     **NO**

Name _____

Grade _____

Homeroom/adviser _____

# IN THE CLASSROOM

22

# ASSET-A-MONTH CALENDAR FOR K-3

**KEY USER/S**
Teachers of grades: K–3

**ASSET CATEGORY**
All

**ASSETS ADDRESSED**
#1, Family Support
#7, Community Values Youth
#11, Family Boundaries
#17, Creative Activities
#21, Achievement Motivation
#26, Caring
#33, Interpersonal Competence
#38, Self-Esteem

## HOW TO USE THIS HANDOUT

For each month of the school year, post one asset category in the classroom. Make your own posters or ask the students to contribute their artistic talents to make a poster for each month. During the month, ask the children to respond to the question on the handout that is associated with the asset of the month. Children can write an answer or draw a picture. Display the writings and drawings on a special assets bulletin board reserved just for this purpose.

## KEEP THIS IN MIND

Search Institute has identified a framework of 40 developmental assets for elementary-age children (ages 6 to 11) that blend Search Institute's research on developmental assets for adolescents with research on healthy child development. Children in grades K–3 can learn about the assets and begin to identify some of the assets they already have in their lives. (Teachers might simplify the language and refer to assets as "good things," as described in *Martin's Good Things,* the children's book available from Search Institute.) Teachers can also sow the seeds for students in K–3 so that from a young age, children intuitively know and seek sources of support.

## NOTES:

# ASSET-A-MONTH CALENDAR FOR K–3

*Once a month, post a new asset category on a bulletin board or wall, explain the category, and ask students to write or draw a response to the following questions:*

**Month 1—Support**
Who loves you and takes care of you? Who can you go to for help or to talk to when you have a question or a problem?

**Month 2—Empowerment**
What are the good things people say about you? Why?

**Month 3—Boundaries and Expectations**
What are two family rules you have to follow? Who are you supposed to tell when you go outside?

**Month 4—Constructive Use of Time**
What do you most like to do? Play an instrument? Play baseball? Read? Act out plays? Sing? How much time do you spend doing that each week?

**Month 5—Commitment to Learning**
Do you want to do well in school and be a good student? Why?

**Month 6—Positive Values**
Do you like to help people? Why?

**Month 7—Social Competencies**
When someone else gets hurt, how do you feel? What does it mean to be a good friend?

**Month 8—Positive Identity**
What good things would the world miss if you weren't here?

# ASSET-A-MONTH CALENDAR FOR 4–6

**KEY USER/S**
Teachers of grades: 4–6

**ASSET CATEGORY**
All

**ASSETS ADDRESSED**
#2, Positive Family Communication
#8, Youth as Resources
#12, School Boundaries
#18, Youth Programs
#22, School Engagement
#27, Equality and Social Justice
#28, Integrity
#33, Interpersonal Competence
#37, Personal Power

## HOW TO USE THIS HANDOUT

For each month of the school year, post one asset category in the classroom. Make your own posters or ask the students to create a poster for each month. During the month, ask the students to respond to the question on the handout that is associated with the asset of the month. They can write an answer or draw a picture. Display the writings and drawings on a special assets bulletin board reserved just for this purpose.

## NOTES:

## KEEP THIS IN MIND

Students in grades 4–6 are developing a sense of themselves in relation to the world around them. Now is the time to build assets for and with these young people. They are developmentally mature enough to start work in earnest on most if not all of the assets.

# ASSET-A-MONTH CALENDAR FOR 4–6

*Once a month, post a new asset category on a bulletin board or wall, explain the category, and ask students to write or draw a response to the following questions:*

**Month 1—Support**
Who can you go to for help or to talk to when you have a question or a problem?

**Month 2—Empowerment**
Do you have a job you do in your neighborhood or community that helps someone else? What is it?

**Month 3—Boundaries and Expectations**
What are three school rules you have to follow? What happens if you break each of these rules?

**Month 4—Constructive Use of Time**
What groups do you do things with? Are you a member of a club, sports team, dance class, scout troop, or other group?

**Month 5—Commitment to Learning**
What do you like to do most at school? What do you wish you could do more of?

**Month 6—Positive Values**
Do you know how many hungry and poor people are in the world? How does that make you feel? What would you like to do about it?

**Month 7—Social Competencies**
What is the most important thing about being a good friend? How do you show your friends that you care about them?

**Month 8—Positive Identity**
Can you change what happens to you? Think of a time when you did something positive that changed what happened next.

**24**

# ASSET-A-MONTH CALENDAR FOR 6–8

**KEY USER/S**
Teachers of grades 6–8

**ASSET CATEGORY**
All

**ASSETS ADDRESSED**
#3, Other Adult Relationships
#9, Service to Others
#14, Adult Role Models
#17, Creative Activities
#23, Homework
#28, Integrity
#36, Peaceful Conflict Resolution
#38, Self-Esteem

## KEEP THIS IN MIND

Students in grades 6–8 are in the critical and sometimes turbulent middle school years. There are all kinds of pressures to fit in, make friends, and make choices that won't embarrass them in front of their peers. Asset building can help make the difference between a difficult and a good middle school experience. Now is the time to engage students in every way and guide them to use their time positively.

## HOW TO USE THIS HANDOUT

For each month of the school year, post one asset category in the classroom. Use the *In Our Own Words* posters available through Search Institute, make your own posters, or sponsor a competition for the best poster for each month. During the month, ask the students to respond to the question on the handout that is associated with the asset of the month. Set aside some time once a week during advisory or homeroom for students to share their responses. Give them the freedom to write, draw, or act out their responses—whatever moves them!

## NOTES:

# ASSET-A-MONTH CALENDAR FOR 6–8

*Once a month, post a new asset category on a bulletin board or wall, explain the category, and ask students to write or draw a response to the questions below. The following statement can be used to help students understand the developmental assets framework:*

"The developmental assets are the opportunities, skills, relationships, values, and self-perceptions that all young people need to succeed. The eight categories of assets are Support, Empowerment, Boundaries and Expectations, Constructive Use of Time, Commitment to Learning, Positive Values, Social Competencies, and Positive Identity."

**Month 1—Support**
What other adults (not a parent or guardian) do you like to be with and can talk to when you have a question or problem?

**Month 2—Empowerment**
What could you do in your neighborhood that would help someone out?

**Month 3—Boundaries and Expectations**
What adult do you know whom you want to be like? Why do you want to be like that person?

**Month 4—Constructive Use of Time**
Are you a member of a faith community? Which one? What creative activities do you like to do? Are you involved in music, theater, or other arts? What do you enjoy about your favorite creative activities?

**Month 5—Commitment to Learning**
How much homework do you have each day after school? Do you get your homework done on time? Do you think it's important to get your homework done and turned in on time? Why?

**Month 6—Positive Values**
If someone was doing something you knew was wrong, would you tell her or him to stop? Would that be hard to do? Why?

**Month 7—Social Competencies**
What's the best way to deal with anger? How can you resolve conflict with someone else in a peaceful way?

**Month 8—Positive Identity**
Do you like yourself? Do you believe that you're a good person?

**25**

# ASSET-A-MONTH CALENDAR FOR 9–12

**KEY USER/S**
Teachers of grades 9–12

**ASSET CATEGORY**
All

**ASSETS ADDRESSED**
#5, Caring School Climate
#9, Service to Others
#15, Positive Peer Influence
#20, Time at Home
#24, Bonding to School
#25, Reading for Pleasure
#28, Integrity
#35, Resistance Skills
#40, Positive View of Personal Future

## KEEP THIS IN MIND

High school students are ready both developmentally and cognitively to do some serious asset-building work. They are ready to take on more complex issues and engage in activities on their own initiative such as service projects. Schools can tap into their energy and help them build assets by structuring some asset-building opportunities.

## HOW TO USE THIS HANDOUT

Structure asset building for high school students by focusing each month of the school year on one or two assets within each category. This can be done in advisory or homeroom, in health/wellness classes, or in social studies classes. Post one asset category in the classroom. Use the *In Our Own Words* posters available through Search Institute, make your own posters, or ask students to make them. During the month, ask the students to respond to the question(s) on the handout that is associated with the asset of the month. Set aside some time once a week for students to share their responses. Encourage students to be creative in their responses—acting, drawing, writing, art/photography, or video.

## NOTES:

# ASSET-A-MONTH CALENDAR FOR 9-12

*Once a month, post a new asset category on a bulletin board or wall, explain the category, and ask students to write or draw a response to the questions below. The following statement can be used to help students understand the developmental assets framework:*

"The developmental assets are the opportunities, skills, relationships, values, and self-perceptions that all young people need to succeed. The eight categories of assets are Support, Empowerment, Boundaries and Expectations, Constructive Use of Time, Commitment to Learning, Positive Values, Social Competencies, and Positive Identity."

### Month 1—Support
What adult in your school do you like to be with and can talk to when you have a question or problem?

### Month 2—Empowerment
What problems do you see in the community?

### Month 3—Boundaries and Expectations
Who are the friends you like the most? What do you admire about them?

### Month 4—Constructive Use of Time
Do you like to spend time at home? How do you most like to spend the time when you're at home and don't have schoolwork to do?

### Month 5—Commitment to Learning
What do you like most about your school? How much time do you spend reading each day or each week? Do you like to read? Do you think you should read more? Why?

### Month 6—Positive Values
Have you ever told the truth about something when it was hard to do that? Tell us that story.

What does responsibility mean? What do you feel responsible for?

### Month 7—Social Competencies
If a friend did something you knew wasn't right, what would you do? How would you do it so you and that person could still be friends?

### Month 8—Positive Identity
Are you optimistic about your personal future? When you look ahead, what do you see for yourself?

# STUDENT STARS

**KEY USER/S**
School administrators, staff

**ASSET CATEGORY**
Support

**ASSETS ADDRESSED**
#5, Caring School Climate

## KEEP THIS IN MIND

How many students feel connected to at least one adult in your school? How many don't feel connected at all? It can be hard to get a true picture of the depth and breadth of student-adult bonds within a school or grade. But finding those students who feel isolated is critical to the health and well-being of the student as well as the school. You can figure out which students may feel isolated or distant from the school community with just a little time and a package of self-sticking stars.

## HOW TO USE THIS HANDOUT

At the start of the school year, put the names of the students in a given class or grade on a wall. Ask school staff (all adults who interact with students) to put a star by the name of each student that adult has a special connection with—students they can identify without having to think about it for very long. Ask every adult in the school to do this, including school bus drivers, custodians, principals, office staff, and food service workers. When all the stars have been placed, find the students with no stars by their names. Begin an invisible friend or mentoring program in which each of these students is assigned to one adult who will work hard to make that special connection. (See handout 18, "Invisible Mentors," for more information.) Try to schedule a follow-up time, maybe during a staff meeting, for people to tell others how it's going and to share ideas about what works and what doesn't in building stronger ties with students. Here's a real example:

## Reaching Out to the Forgotten Half in Georgetown, Texas

All kids are our kids. Principal Randy Adair at Benold Middle School in Georgetown, Texas, decided to put that theory to the test. During a staff-planning meeting he posted on the walls of the school cafeteria a list of all 900 students. "I gave each teacher ten stickers and asked them

to put a star next to the students that they had the closest relationship to," says Adair.

After the task was completed, teachers and staff members were shocked to discover that while a quarter of the students had a number of stars

*cont.* ▶

# PASS IT ON **AT SCHOOL!**

next to their names, more than half of the students didn't have any stickers at all. "I asked the teachers to put stars next to the names of the kids whom they would like to start relationships with in some way," says Adair. Then the teachers were charged with finding small ways to connect to the student without necessarily drawing attention to the fact that they were doing so. The goal was to build bridges to the youth, especially those in high-risk situations that made learning and bonding to the school community difficult. "To start, it could be as simple as saying 'hi' to a young person in the hall," he says.

Sixth-grade teacher Mindy Ellerbee says that this new school philosophy has made a difference in her classroom. "I've found that by talking about the assets and raising the level of respect, students put more effort into their work than ever before," she says. "I believe it's because they get a sense that teachers care."

Story adapted from "Every student a star: School staff reach out to the forgotten half," by Kalisha Davis. Found in *Assets: The Magazine of Ideas for Healthy Communities and Healthy Youth*, Spring 2000.

# STUDENT STARS

My "star" student is

My commitment is to create a special connection with this student by:

1.

2.

3.

Here are some ideas for getting started. Circle the ones you'd like to try with your "star" student.

- Make eye contact and use the student's name or nickname in daily greetings.
- Learn something about the student: What does he/she like or hate to do? What talents or interests does he/she have?
- Find out what's going on in the student's life. Find out about her/his family. Ask about problems he/she may be experiencing.
- Attend a game, play, tournament, or other activity the student is involved in.
- Offer to help with homework, lab work, or a special project.
- Encourage the student to ask for help when he or she needs it. Make yourself available after school sometimes, if necessary.
- Stay in touch on special occasions such as birthdays, holidays, and vacation breaks.

# THE STORY OF ME!

> **KEY USER/S**
> School staff
>
> **ASSET CATEGORY**
> Empowerment
>
> **ASSETS ADDRESSED**
> #7, Community Values Youth

## KEEP THIS IN MIND

Give students a chance to shine! Young people who feel they are known and accepted for who they are also feel that others value them. One fast way to develop students' sense of value is to create a way for them to tell their stories. Take that one step further to publishing those stories and you've created an opportunity for students to feel that they are important—in the classroom and in the larger school community.

## HOW TO USE THIS HANDOUT

The opportunity for students to tell their stories can be created in classes, such as advisory, history, English/literature, and health, or in small groups conducted by school counselors or social workers. The activity handout can be used to help students get started and give shape to their narratives. Once the stories are down on paper, you can create an opportunity for sharing those stories in a number of ways.

- Ask students to pair up and exchange and read each other's stories. Then have each student introduce the other to the class, using information from that student's story.

- Collect the stories, delete the names, and hand them out randomly. Ask each student to read the story out loud. After each reading, ask the class to guess which student's story has just been read. The guessing game can be both fun and poignant, leaving students with a deeper understanding and appreciation of their classmates.

- Help the students edit their written stories to a one-page length and into something the student is comfortable seeing in print. Have students assemble the stories into a book that is duplicated and given to each student in the class or group.

- Select portions of the students' stories that reflect specific assets, group those selections together, and ask students to read them out loud in class. Students may be surprised to learn about the many strengths their classmates currently have.

## NOTES:

# THE STORY OF ME!

Hi! My name is

These are the things I'm really good at:

_____

_____

_____

One time I really helped someone by:

_____

_____

_____

And this is how it happened:

_____

_____

_____

One time I learned something important about myself. This is how it happened:

_____

_____

_____

_____

**27**

And this is what I discovered about myself:

_____

_____

_____

_____

What I'd like to change in my life right now is:

_____

_____

_____

_____

What I like about my life right now is:

_____

_____

_____

_____

Is it okay for others to read this
or for the teacher to read this out loud? (CIRCLE ONE.)

### YES    NO    PLEASE TALK TO ME FIRST.

**28**

# QUICK CHECK FOR STUDENT ASSETS

**KEY USER/S**
Teachers

**ASSET CATEGORY**
All

**ASSETS ADDRESSED**
All

**NOTES:**

## KEEP THIS IN MIND

Knowing where to go usually depends on where you are. To help your students build assets, you need to know what assets they have and what assets they need to develop. Teachers can get a good classroom-sized glimpse of what their students' asset strengths and needs are by asking them to do a quick self-assessment.

## HOW TO USE THIS HANDOUT

Give students a list of the 40 assets (Activity Handout 1) and ask them to think about what assets they feel they already have, what assets they have but need to strengthen, and what assets they really don't possess in their lives at the moment. Distribute the handout and ask the students to record this information (without putting their name on the sheet), along with some things they can do right now to start strengthening their asset base. Gather and tally the responses to create a quick classroom assets profile. Share the results with the students.

# QUICK CHECK FOR STUDENT ASSETS
## MY PERSONALIZED ASSET PROFILE

At this moment, my three strongest assets are:

1. _____

2. _____

3. _____

Assets I have but need to strengthen include:

1. _____

2. _____

3. _____

Three assets I don't have going for me and need to develop are:

1. _____

2. _____

3. _____

These are some things I can/will do to strengthen my assets:

1. _____

2. _____

3. _____

**29**

# STAND UP AND SPEAK OUT

## KEEP THIS IN MIND

If you want to engage students, ask them what they think. Adults who ask questions and listen to the answers can be magnets for students who need to feel that their thoughts are important. Students, especially younger ones, don't necessarily have the confidence to stand up and speak out, and many aren't sure how to express what they think. Teachers can create an open, accepting culture within the classroom that invites students to share ideas. Teachers can also help students be more willing to articulate their ideas by listening to them and then rephrasing what they have said. The rephrasing will teach students ways to state their case and help others understand and respond to the ideas expressed.

## HOW TO USE THIS HANDOUT

Teachers can encourage students to stand up and speak out by asking them to discuss personal values. Teachers can use these guidelines:

- Engage students in conversations about priorities, choices, and personal values.

- Provide opportunities to stand up for one's beliefs and act on convictions.

- Promote understanding and acceptance of differences.

- Celebrate having an "internal compass" that guides actions.

## NOTES:

# STAND UP AND SPEAK OUT

If you want to engage students, ask them what they think. Adults who ask questions and listen to the answers can be magnets for students who need to feel that their thoughts are important. Teachers can create an open, accepting culture within the classroom that invites students to share opinions. Here are some ideas for discussion:

- Which is more important, family or friends?
- Is education important as a way to learn and enrich the experience of living or as a way to make more money?
- How important is money to being happy?
- If you see someone being hurt (either physically or verbally), should you intervene even if you might get hurt yourself?
- Does it matter that people in our world are poor and hungry?
- How should governments handle overpopulation in the world? Why is it a problem?
- What should we do about pollution in the environment?

Ask the students to come up with topics of interest to them and record them here:

- _____

- _____

- _____

## DISCUSSION SETTINGS

- Set up a general class discussion, with the teacher or a student as moderator.
- Pose a question and ask two students or two groups of students to take a side and present it to the class.
- Split the class in two and ask each group to study and present a side by writing paragraphs or short papers. Ask for volunteers to read their papers, alternating sides. Allow for all-class discussion after every four or so papers have been read.
- For younger students, ask them to draw pictures that show how they feel about a particular topic. Post the pictures, grouping them on two separate bulletin boards. Ask the students to take time to look over all the pictures and then have a class discussion about how they reacted to the various pictures.
- Play charades. Pose a values question and ask individual students or groups of students to act out their stance on that question.

# WHAT DO YOU WANT TO LEARN?

## KEEP THIS IN MIND

Educators can become good at building relationships with students by sometimes stepping out of the routine. Students and teachers who work together on projects or activities that are new or outside of the typical roles often experience each other in new and exciting ways. Teachers can be on the lookout for cocurricular activities that give them another way of relating to students and a chance to show support for the importance of youth programs in school success.

## HOW TO USE THIS HANDOUT

Teachers can use the handout as a planning tool to create an activity and structure it to ensure student success. The handout will help teachers engage students in creating activities that are meaningful to them and motivate them to get the most from the activity as they gain skills and help each other. Choose activities that are personal and inviting. Be informal and flexible to ensure that the activity is more meaningful for the students.

**Use the following to help you organize this activity:**

These are the activities I have in mind:

_____

_____

These are the suggestions my students have provided:

_____

_____

# PASS IT ON **AT SCHOOL!**

## TIPS FOR USING **Activity Handout 30**

Is there a way to make the activity more personal for the students?

_____

_____

This is how I will encourage intellectual curiosity and motivate students to ask questions:

_____

_____

These are the skills I want the students to gain:

_____

_____

This is how I will connect the skills and learning to real life:

_____

_____

**30**

# WHAT DO YOU WANT TO LEARN?

**If you had the chance to pick a topic our class would talk or learn about for one week, what would it be? Write your top three suggestions below or draw a picture of each one.**

**1.**

**2.**

**3.**

# EXPECT THE BEST

---

**KEY USER/S**
Teachers, other school staff

**ASSET CATEGORY**
Boundaries and Expectations

**ASSETS ADDRESSED**
#12, School Boundaries
#16, High Expectations

---

## KEEP THIS IN MIND

Students perform best when the school provides clear rules and consequences and when teachers and other school staff encourage them to do and be their best. Teachers and other school staff are frequently the adults in students' lives who most affect them during the school-age years and later in life. Give young people boundaries and expect excellence from each and every student.

## HOW TO USE THIS HANDOUT

This following handout is designed to be posted as a daily reminder to help teachers and staff establish limits that tell students what is expected of them. Giving them boundaries and having high expectations for them gives students the chance to succeed. After all, they need to know the rules of the game in order to win at it. And when young people are expected to be and do their best, they are their best. Teachers and staff can copy and post the Expect the Best list by their desks, on the bathroom mirror, on the dashboard of the car or bus—wherever it can serve as a daily reminder of ways to help students achieve.

## NOTES:

**31**

# EXPECT THE BEST

To create a respectful, supportive, two-way relationship with my students I will:

- Work with them to create rules and norms about appropriate behavior in the classroom.

- Tell them what I expect.

- Ask them what they expect of me.

- Be consistent by firmly enforcing the agreed-upon rules.

- Use visual, auditory, and tactile reminders about boundaries.

- Model the behavior I expect from my students.

- Show students respect, leadership, and participation and invite them to use those behaviors, too.

- Set high and realistic expectations for my students.

- Trust my students to do the best they can.

- Help my students redefine perfectionism—it's not doing something perfectly that counts, but doing as well as each student can.

- Never give up on them.

*Contributed by Marilyn Peplau, Search Institute trainer and consultant for Vision Training Associates.*

# LET'S DO IT!

## KEEP THIS IN MIND

Schools can develop ways for special education students to make meaningful contributions to the school community and their fellow students. Providing service to others empowers students and helps them build self-esteem. It also creates a two-way street that invites positive interaction and connection with the rest of the school.

## HOW TO USE THIS HANDOUT

Ask the students for their ideas about ways they can provide a service or do something to make the school a better place. Help them think of ideas by listing categories of possible ways to help. Read some of the suggestions on the handout as idea starters. Write ideas on the board, and then have the students vote on the idea they like best. Once the group agrees on *what* they want to do, work with them to figure out *how*. Help them settle on a simple idea that is easy to do, and break down how to do it into small, easy-to-achieve steps. Find ways to invite the general student population to help. Plan a pizza party or root beer float toast to celebrate the activity or project after finishing.

## NOTES:

# LET'S DO IT!

What are the things that we can do to make our school a
better place for everyone? **HERE ARE SOME IDEAS:**

· Attend local games, plays, and other activities sponsored by the
  school to show school spirit.

· Sponsor a schoolwide educational program that teaches the student
  population how to be more supportive of people with disabilities.

· Sponsor a fun activity like a floor decorating contest or game night.

· Create an award to present in recognition of other youth and adults who
  make the school community better.

· Invite students to help with adopted sports teams.

· Help younger children in lower grades.

· Hold a fund-raiser such as a cookie, bake, or candy sale and donate the
  money to a local charity.

## OTHER IDEAS:

· 

· 

·

# LITTLE BIG THINGS

**NOTES:**

## KEEP THIS IN MIND

Busy teachers and staff members often feel that they can't add one more thing to their plates. Asset building may sound to some like another thing to add to the workload. But the truth is that many asset-building techniques are simple, quick, and easy to do.

## HOW TO USE THIS HANDOUT

Staff members can use the handout as a mini-refresher course in the little things they can do to help students develop assets. Many of these "little big things" will also serve to help students build positive self-concepts.  Staff won't be able to do all of these things, but they might find a few ideas they can use that make sense within the realities of their particular classroom setting. Post the handout where it will be seen at the start of each day—in the staff lounge, in the office, or in the staff bathrooms!

# LITTLE BIG THINGS

**Little Big Things to do for students every day:**

- Greet students at the door.

- Speak to or call each student by name in your class each day.

- Notice things about students that show you care and are interested in them as people.

- Make positive statements as often as possible.

- Dispute only inaccurate facts and accept opinions even though they may differ from yours.

- Provide opportunities for students to have some control in the learning environment (such as selection of course content or ways of teaching/learning).

- Smile more.

- Give students responsibility and think of them as responsible and resourceful people.

- Be honest with students—their trust in you is tied to your trust in them.

- Express anger toward a misbehavior rather than toward a student or group of students.

- Stay in the present—learn to forgive and forget.

- Be authentic—be a real person to students.

- Encourage students to be problem solvers and then *accept and honor their solutions.*

- Go to a student event outside the classroom to show your interest and support.

- Become adept at cooperative learning as a teaching strategy—it gives *all* students purpose and opportunities to participate in meaningful ways.

- Use a student-led parent-teacher conference model. (See activity handout 34, "Student-Led Conferences.")

- Sponsor a student club or activity.

- Structure learning around mastery rather than grades.

- Make yourself available to students at a consistent time each day.

- Never use sarcasm with students—it can damage any relationship.

- Monitor your conversation in the teachers' lounge—does it affirm students?

- Pay attention to building your own assets and positive self-concept.

*Contributed by Christine Beyer, Search Institute trainer and consultant for Vision Training Associates.*

# STUDENT-LED CONFERENCES

**KEY USER/S**
Teachers

**ASSET CATEGORY**
Positive Values, Positive Identity

**ASSETS ADDRESSED**
#30, Responsibility
#37, Personal Power

## KEEP THIS IN MIND

What better way to talk about student challenges and progress with parents than to ask the students! Teachers often spend a great deal of time preparing for parent-teacher conferences. Invite students to help you organize. Students know themselves better than anyone else does. Asking students to participate in assessing their own issues, strengths, and goals shifts the responsibility from teachers and parents to the students themselves.

## HOW TO USE THIS HANDOUT

During the week before parent-teacher conferences, give students the following handout. If possible, give them time to fill it out in the classroom. Collect the handouts and have them available for the conferences. Ask students to lead the conference discussion by reading what they've written in each discussion area. Note: Relatively young students can be asked to do this as well. Expect students to need some coaching from you about how to lead the discussion.

**NOTES:**

# STUDENT-LED CONFERENCES

## STUDENT CONFERENCE NOTES

What are you good at? Do you have any strengths in particular that you've noticed in the past semester? (Name at least one strength.)

What challenges do you have? Have you noticed any particular challenges in the past semester?

What are three goals you'd like to work toward during the next semester?

1. _____

2. _____

3. _____

How can we (parents and teachers) help you with those goals?

# ADULTS GET ANGRY, TOO!

**KEY USER/S**
Teachers, school staff

**ASSET CATEGORY**
Support, Empowerment, Social
Competencies

**ASSETS ADDRESSED**
#5, Caring School Climate
#10, Safety
#36, Peaceful Conflict Resolution

## KEEP THIS IN MIND

Managing angry feelings is not just something
students need to do—teachers and other school
staff get angry, too. To nurture a caring and safe
school climate, adults who interact with students
must handle conflicts calmly and in ways that
always show respect for students.

## HOW TO USE THIS HANDOUT

This handout will help teachers and other school
staff transform situations that involve conflict
with students into opportunities to build assets
with and for students.

**NOTES:**

# ADULTS GET ANGRY, TOO!

## FROM ANGER MANAGEMENT TO ASSET DEVELOPMENT

The following scenarios are paired with suggestions for developing assets. These pairings provide ideas about alternative ways to handle your own anger.

| CONFLICT SCENARIO | ASSET-BUILDING APPROACH |
|---|---|
| A student continually speaks out of turn in class, talking to and distracting other students while you're trying to teach. She ignores your direct requests to quiet down. | Give the student an active role in the classroom—pass out papers, facilitate a discussion group, be the spokesperson for a pro/con debate. |
| A fight breaks out between two students in the cafeteria. The students are separated but continue to verbally lash out at each other and you. | Work with each student separately. Involve each in a service project that requires empathy—mentor physically disabled students, coach an adaptive sport, be a buddy to a student in a younger grade. |
| A student blatantly disrespects or says something derogatory about another staff member within your hearing. | Ask the student involved to make an apology to the staff member toward whom her or his comments were directed. Then engage the young person in a service-learning opportunity or find some other way for her or him to be of service in the school community. |

Write other scenarios you have had to deal with and suggest asset-building ways to respond.

| CONFLICT SCENARIO | ASSET-BUILDING APPROACH |
|---|---|
|  |  |
|  |  |
|  |  |

# SMOOTH TRANSITIONS

**KEY USER/S**
Teachers, guidance counselors, social workers

**ASSET CATEGORY**
Support, Social Competencies

**ASSETS ADDRESSED**
#2, Positive Family Communication
#3, Other Adult Relationships
#32, Planning and Decision Making

## KEEP THIS IN MIND

Transitions from elementary to middle school and middle school to high school can be hard for many students. Young people face big changes in teachers, schools, and friends while sensing that more will be expected of them. Two things can help students make their transition with less worry and more confidence: the support of key adults who will help them make the move and the encouragement to plan ahead and make choices.

## HOW TO USE THIS HANDOUT

You can use the handout to help students moving to middle school or high school think through their anxieties and fears. The handout also aids students in creating an action plan to get the support they need for a successful transition. You can ask students to fill out the handout and choose one adult with whom they will share this information. You can also be the designated "trusted adult" and talk individually with students.

## NOTES:

# SMOOTH TRANSITIONS

1. When I think about my upcoming move into middle or high school, these are the things I am most concerned about (examples include: leaving friends; making new friends; not knowing the building, rules, and routines; being bullied or pressured to use drugs):

    Concerns I have:

    1. _____

    2. _____

    3. _____

2. I know one or more adults whom I feel I could talk with about my concerns. These are the adults I can depend on to help me (this might be a parent, teacher, neighbor, coach, or other school staff person):

    Adults I can talk with:

    1. _____

    2. _____

    3. _____

3. I asked one of the adults I listed above to help me with my problem and figure out the best way to handle it. These are the ideas that we came up with:

    Solutions:

    1. _____

    2. _____

    3. _____

# WHAT DO I HAVE GOING FOR ME? (TWO-PART HANDOUT)

**KEY USER/S**
Teachers

**ASSET CATEGORY**
Support, Boundaries and Expectations, Positive Values

**ASSETS ADDRESSED**
#5, Caring School Climate
#12, School Boundaries
#16, High Expectations
#30, Responsibility

## KEEP THIS IN MIND

Teachers can use asset building to address a student's problem behavior by confronting it squarely the first time. By encouraging positive behavior and offering students an opportunity to express their opinions, teachers can help students see their value and the value of others.

## HOW TO USE THIS HANDOUT

The following handouts give responsibility back to students for knowing who they are, what they need, and what steps they need to take to stop the problem behavior. Ask students to review the list of 40 assets (Activity Handout 1) and consider how their actions can influence school climate/community. Ask them to read the first handout and to either fill it in or talk it through with you. The second handout serves as a con- tract shared between the student and the school community. Strongly encourage the students to create their own positive action steps by asking them to write out some goals for change, sign the form, and commit to a follow-up visit with you.

## NOTES:

# WHAT DO I HAVE GOING FOR ME?

## Part 1: Why Am I Here?

Take a moment to reflect on the following questions and fill in as much information as you can.

The situation that brought me here today is:

What happened? What did you say or do? What did others say or do? Write or draw a picture.

If I had the chance to do it over, I would do things differently. *(Circle one.)*  **Yes    No**
Why?

What are some things you normally do to make school a better place? (Write down things such as respecting other people, helping others, or playing a sport.)

What are the things you'd like to improve on if you had help from someone whom you could trust?

What do you need to see or hear to feel as if you are supported by the students and adults here at school?

# WHAT DO I HAVE GOING FOR ME?

## Part 2: Contract for Change

You have already been asked to fill out the form "Why Am I Here?" Now we are asking that you fill out the "Contract for Change." This is a commitment to intentionally work toward making our school a better place for everyone. You can do this by acting positively, being a good influence on others, and taking responsibility for yourself. Think about the things that you can do and write your ideas below. Remember, you don't have to do this by yourself. It is our responsibility to make sure that you have the support you need to reach your goals.

Date _____ Name _____

Grade _____ Adviser _____

A brief explanation of what happened:

Goals you will work on to create a safer, more caring school for everyone:

    Goals                                      Completed on

    1. _____     _____

    2. _____     _____

    3. _____     _____

Date to report back _____

Person to whom you will report _____

# IN THE STAFF MEETING

# EVERYONE COUNTS!

**38**

KEY USER/S
Administrators

ASSET CATEGORY
Support

ASSETS ADDRESSED
#3, Other Adult Relationships
#5, Caring School Climate

## KEEP THIS IN MIND

Every adult in the school is important in the life of the student. Office staff, custodians, and security staff are important in setting the tone for a welcoming, safe school climate. Many are already natural asset builders and need recognition of their efforts and successes in connecting with students. Others can be asset builders but need the confidence—and permission—to try. Principals should make sure to include office staff, custodians, and security staff in schoolwide asset-building efforts and acknowledge them publicly and frequently for their successes.

## HOW TO USE THIS HANDOUT

Use the following handout to give school office, custodial, and security staff ideas for ways to make a difference in students' lives. Copy and distribute the handout individually, at all-staff meetings, or in asset-building teaching sessions set up especially for this important group of potential asset builders. Or, make posters from the handout and put them up where these staff members will see them daily. Another alternative is to put up Search Institute posters—*40 Ways to Show You Care* or *You Can*—in the school office, staff lounge, and break rooms. Emphasize the idea that *everyone counts*, everyone has a contribution to make, and everyone has the ability to be an asset builder.

## NOTES:

38

# EVERYONE COUNTS!
## BE PART OF A STUDENT'S SUCCESS— BE AN ASSET BUILDER!

*Greet students.* Learn as many students' names as possible, call them by their names, say "hello" and "good-bye," and make eye contact.

*Ask questions.* Find out something about each student you come into contact with.

*Invite discussion.* Ask students how they are or how their days are going.

*Listen.* When you ask a question, *hear* the answer! Listen to what young people have to say—their insights are genuine and often unique.

*Interact.* Find ways to interact with students beyond just greeting them. Give out holiday treats, go out of your way to follow up on a discussion, or meet a need.

*Reward positive behavior.* Catch students doing something right, report it, and reward it.

## HERE ARE SOME EXAMPLES OF ASSET BUILDING MAKING A REAL DIFFERENCE!

The custodians at one school keep a special candy dish in their break room that all the students know about. Students can take the special candy (they call it "moon rocks") by invitation only. The custodians single out students they happen to be talking with or students who help them out and invite them to go get a handful of moon rocks.  Occasionally, on special holidays or for other events, whole classes are invited to the break room for special-event moon rocks.

A security staff member at another school gave high fives to students who told him their names as they passed by him each morning. The ritual became contagious so that students were often backed up in a line that filed past the high-five-slapping guard!

**39**

# TOO MUCH, TOO LITTLE

## KEEP THIS IN MIND

It's a fact. Teachers have too many issues to deal
with and too little time to address them. Their
workload is often heavy, demands are pressing,
and the needs of the students they teach seem
overwhelming. Schools can lift some of the bur-
den by redirecting some challenges to others,
particularly to parents, volunteers, and community, business, and neighborhood partnerships.
School administrators can ask teachers to identify their most time-consuming challenges. A
little thinking outside the box may lead schools
to solutions that engage outside resources, help
build student assets, and relieve some of the
pressure on one of their most valuable resources—their teachers.

## HOW TO USE THIS HANDOUT

At a staff meeting, distribute the handout and
ask teachers to return it before the next meeting. Study the responses. List all the challenges
teachers reported and identify the top three or
four. Distribute the results in the form of a short
report to everyone in the school—administrators, teachers, school board members, students,
parents, volunteers, office and custodial staff,
food service workers, and bus drivers. Provide
an idea box in the office and ask them to offer
ideas they may have to bring in outside resources
to help. Use their ideas to develop partnerships,
create a broader volunteer base, draw on corpo-
rate or business resources, and engage parents
and other community partners.

## NOTES:

# TOO MUCH, TOO LITTLE

Teachers have many issues to deal with and little time to deal with them. The school administration is looking for ways to invite outside resources to help with some of these challenges. But first we need to know what challenges each of you face and, of those, which you consider to be most pressing. Please take a moment to answer these three questions and return your responses to the office. You do not need to identify yourself. We will use this information to develop a plan to take a little off your plates.

1. List the issues that make your teaching workload difficult (list as many as you can).

2. Of these, which three are the most pressing?

3. What do you think might help relieve the more pressing issues?

**Thank you for taking time to give us your thoughts!**

**40**

# ASSET BUILDER OF THE MONTH

---

**KEY USER/S**
Administrators, teachers, staff, students

**ASSET CATEGORY**
Support

**ASSETS ADDRESSED**
#5, Caring School Climate

---

## KEEP THIS IN MIND

While primary asset-building efforts focus on students, don't forget the teachers and staff! Students need recognition, and that recognition motivates them to do more with assets—and the same is true for teachers and other school staff. School administrators need to learn about asset-building efforts taken on by specific teachers and find ways to publicly acknowledge those teachers and support those activities. When many teachers buy into and work on asset building, this can help build a caring school climate, which in turn, becomes another key asset for students.

## HOW TO USE THIS HANDOUT

At faculty or student organization meetings, distribute the handout and ask teachers to nominate an asset builder of the month. Nominations can be limited to teaching staff or opened up to all school staff. Create a tradition of naming the Asset Builder of the Month at staff meetings or school assemblies, or acknowledge that person and explain her or his achievements in a school newsletter, on the school Web site, or on a special bulletin board.

## NOTES:

40

# ASSET BUILDER OF THE MONTH

**Is there a member of the staff who does a great job building assets with and for students? Write her or his name below and tell us why you think our school community should recognize her or him.**

I would like to nominate _____

This is why I think my nominee deserves to be Asset Builder of the Month:

# FIRST STEPS

**41**

---

**KEY USER/S**
All school staff

**ASSET CATEGORY**
All

**ASSETS ADDRESSED**
All

## KEEP THIS IN MIND

School staff members often wonder what they can do as individuals to get the asset-building process rolling. Some feel that there's nothing they can do on their own to change the school climate or introduce assets. Just knowing the basic steps can help individuals develop a shared vision for asset building.

## HOW TO USE THIS HANDOUT

The handout suggests a series of steps that lead to changing the school climate and building assets schoolwide. Use the checklist to reflect personally on the ways you might approach asset building or encourage the school to do so. Add asset building to the agenda at school staff meetings and distribute copies of the checklist to get the discussion rolling.

**NOTES:**

# FIRST STEPS

Use the following as a checklist to think about ways school staff can focus on asset-building strategies that are important to the unique needs of the school.

**Assess current needs.** What do students at our school need and how are those needs being addressed right now? What programs and opportunities are already in place that support asset building? What activities might be developed?

**Build a shared vision.** How can we tap the ideas and energy of the whole school to create a shared vision of the kind of asset building we would like to do and the kind of strengths we would like our students to have?

**Create awareness and commitment.** Start a campaign to reach all school staff to make them aware of how crucial their role is in building student assets. How can we make sure that all adults in the school who interact with our students understand how important they are in this undertaking? Can we form a core group that is committed to moving forward with asset building?

**Nurture the support assets.** The support assets have to do with building people connections—with family, other adults, neighbors, and school. The focus is on helping students develop a broad base of support and break through barriers that isolate and alienate them. What goals can we set, both in the short and long term, to really address and bolster the human connections for our students?

**Empower students through service and leadership.** Service to others is a powerful asset-building tool. How can we encourage service activities within the school and in partnership with outside neighbors, communities, and businesses?

**Involve students in constructive activities.** Students have a lot of free time—sometimes too much! How can we help students avoid unsafe activities and behavior by offering interesting activities, safe places, and creative outlets?

**Nurture positive values.** Students make important choices based on what they value. How can we encourage thoughtful discussion about values like responsibility, honesty, compassion, equality, and respect?

**Develop social competencies and positive identity.** In what ways can we encourage students to build life skills? How can we help them make good decisions, make friends, enjoy healthy self-esteem, relate well to diverse people, and maintain a sense of hope?

**Educate and support parents.** What can we do to support the family—the primary shaping influence in the lives of our students?

**Reach out to the community.** What can we do to reach out to the larger community to create a healthy place for all students?

# IN THE CAFETERIA

# SERVE UP "SOUL FOOD"

**42**

**KEY USER/S**
Food service workers

**ASSET CATEGORY**
Support, Empowerment

**ASSETS ADDRESSED**
#5, Caring School Climate
#8, Youth as Resources

**NOTES:**

## KEEP THIS IN MIND

Like every other adult in the school, food service workers are important asset builders. Food builds students' bodies and assets help build happy, caring adults. Food service workers can serve "soul food" in the cafeteria! Some of the best conversations happen at mealtimes. Food service workers see students in a unique situation—students are more relaxed, the setting is informal, and the mellowing aspect of food is involved. Food service workers have the power to make lunch more than just a simple routine for students.

## HOW TO USE THIS HANDOUT

Food service workers can use the following handout for ideas to strengthen their connections with the students they serve. They can also involve students in cafeteria routines that build assets as well as strong, healthy bodies. If your school doesn't prepare food on-site, consider having a few special activities that are similar to the ideas listed.

# SERVE UP "SOUL FOOD"

You can make a difference! Here are some ideas for building assets with and for students:

- *Make it special.* What can you celebrate? Make special foods or desserts (cookies, anyone?) for special times—homecoming, holidays, prom, graduation, the school musical—or to celebrate team victories or club competitions.

- *Make it theirs.* Appoint a student each week who has the honor of deciding what cookie of the week will be made for the following week. Create a student food service advisory. Appoint a food critic to make the rounds of the cafeteria and post a weekly restaurant review (encourage positive comments as well as critical).

- *Ask for suggestions.* Put out a "recipe box" and invite students to put ideas for what they'd like to see on the menu or recipes for special foods or treats. Make sure to post the name of the student who contributed the idea or recipe on the day that food is served.

- *Ask for help.* Ask students to create colorful menus for days when something special is served or when a particular event is being celebrated.

- *Make it unique.* Celebrate diversity! Ask students for recipes and suggestions for foods that reflect the students' ethnic, racial, and cultural heritages.

- *Invite participation.* Ask the students who supply the recipes or ideas to come to the kitchen to supervise the preparation. Or ask them to invite their parents or grandparents in to consult with you or supervise the food preparation of a special dish.

- *Make it warm.* Greet students, look them in the eye, and ask them questions as they move through the line. When you have time, go "tableside" to talk to students, ask them how the food is, and engage them in conversation.

# TREAT SHEET

**43**

**KEY USER/S**
Food service workers

**ASSET CATEGORY**
Positive Values, Social Competencies

**ASSETS ADDRESSED**
#30, Responsibility
#32, Planning and Decision Making

## KEEP THIS IN MIND

Food service workers can be instrumental in teaching healthy eating habits and general nutrition information. Elementary and middle school students in particular can be influenced by exchanging information for a special treat.

## HOW TO USE THIS HANDOUT

Once a week, food service menus can include a unique or special treat, which students have to earn. Hand out a healthy eating test and give students the treat for turning in completed sheets. Post hints around the cafeteria. Hints might be in the form of:

- Riddles on poster board hung on the cafeteria walls;

- Fill-in-the-blank rhymes indicating a word that answers one of the questions;

- A display of a particular food that answers a test question—for example, a huge pile of apples or fruit in an unusual place; or

- A particular song playing in the background that emphasizes a word or type of food which answers a particular question.

**NOTES:**

# TREAT SHEET

What you are is what you eat! We, the food service staff, challenge you to make good choices about what you eat. But to do that, you need to know a few things. Answer these questions and turn in your Treat Sheet to get the cook's special treat! (Hint: Look around the cafeteria for answers to questions that stump you.)

43

1. Name the three golden rules of good eating habits

a. _____

b. _____

c. _____

2. What is the right approach to healthy eating?

3. What do potato chips, fast-food cheeseburgers, and fries have in common?

4. Circle the foods below that have the least fat:

- Vegetables
- Burgers with cheese and sauce
- Lean meats
- Fish
- Fries
- Poultry without skin
- Cookies and donuts
- Broiled or baked rather than fried foods
- Salads with creamy dressings
- Salads with oil-and-vinegar or light dressings

5. What's that hiding in your soft drink?

6. How can you learn more about and make good choices about what you eat?

---

This article originally appeared in the April 1992 *FDA Consumer* (U.S. Food and Drug Administration), and contains revisions made in April 1995, December 1996, and January 1999.

**43**

---

## ANSWERS TO TREAT SHEET

1. a. Eat your vegetables
   b. Limit sweets.
   c. Drink your milk.

2. Eat a variety of foods from each of these groups:
   - Vegetables
   - Fruits
   - Breads, cereals, rice, and pasta
   - Milk, yogurt, and cheese
   - Meat, poultry, fish, dried beans and peas, eggs, and nuts

3. Fat! Plus sugar and salt—all things you should limit in what you eat.
   Fats are our most concentrated source of energy. Scientists know that eating too much fat, especially saturated fat and cholesterol, increases blood cholesterol levels, and therefore increases your risk of heart disease. Too much fat also may lead to being overweight and increase your risk of some cancers.

4. - Vegetables
   - Lean meats
   - Fish
   - Poultry without skin
   - Broiled or baked rather than fried foods
   - Salads with oil-and-vinegar or light dressings

5. Sugar! It's often in the form of corn syrup. Read the label to find out. Besides sugar, other sweeteners are sometimes "hidden" in foods and added to soft drinks. Sweets can be an additional source of calories, contain only limited nutrients, and contribute to tooth decay.

6. Read the labels! The food label can help nutrition-conscious people make wise food choices.

# CONSIDER THE HUNGRY QUESTIONNAIRE

**KEY USER/S**
Food service workers

**ASSET CATEGORY**
Empowerment, Constructive Use of Time, Positive Values

**ASSETS ADDRESSED**
#9, Service to Others
#18, Youth Programs
#26, Caring
#27, Equality and Social Justice

## KEEP THIS IN MIND

Young people in the United States often have little awareness of how many children in the world suffer the crippling effects of hunger and poverty. As students enjoy a meal in the cafeteria, challenge them not to take that meal for granted. The cafeteria is a great place to begin a food awareness campaign that just may move some students to take action.

## HOW TO USE THIS HANDOUT

Give the Consider the Hungry questionnaire to students as they enter the cafeteria or use the information to make posters to place on the cafeteria walls. But don't stop there—use the Make a Difference suggestions to challenge students to take action. Put a collection box out for cash donations to be given to a food bank, or ask for volunteers to work at a local food bank or holiday shelter meal event. Organize a group of students to work with you to come up with ideas for ways to get students involved in local child hunger/poverty activities.

**NOTES:**

**44**

# CONSIDER THE HUNGRY QUESTIONNAIRE

**44**

**1. How many children in the world die of hunger each day?**

Every day, worldwide, 34,000 children under age 5 die of hunger or preventable diseases resulting from hunger.

**2. How many Americans are too poor to provide enough food for their families?**

A 1995 study by Tufts University estimates that 20 million to 30 million Americans are too poor to meet their monthly expenses and buy enough food to live healthy, productive lives.

**3. How many children in the United States go to bed hungry each night?**

A July 1999 report from the National Center for Children in Poverty found that 1 out of every 8 children under the age of 12 in the United States goes to bed hungry every night.

**4. How many people in the world do you think are hungry?**

World hunger organizations estimate that nearly one billion people around the world are chronically hungry.

**5. Does hunger make a difference in how well young people do in school?**

A June 2002 report by Dr. J. Larry Brown from the Center on Hunger and Poverty found that young people who are hungry miss more days of school and are less prepared to learn when they are able to attend, are less able to learn, repeat grades, and have poorer overall school achievement.

## MAKE A DIFFERENCE

Here are some things that students can do to change the hunger numbers:

- Learn about hunger. Then talk to others about it. The Internet is full of resources to learn more.
- Organize your friends to take action. Find a hunger relief organization (local shelter, food bank, etc.) and ask them how you can help.
- Raise money to give to food banks or other local organizations that specifically help ease hunger among children.
- Share this information with your family, friends, and neighbors. If 1 out of 8 children goes to bed hungry every night and your school has 800 students in it, there could be 100 hungry students in your own school!

# IN THE STAFF LOUNGE

# NEW PERCEPTIONS

**KEY USER/S**
Teachers, administrators, parent organizations, student organizations

**ASSET CATEGORY**
All

**ASSETS ADDRESSED**
All

**45**

## KEEP THIS IN MIND

The asset-building mind-set sometimes means clearing away old ideas about young people. Everyone involved in the school community can cultivate an internal attitude of respect and caring that translates into external improvements in the feel and spirit of the school. Is the glass half full or half empty? Each individual has a choice to make about how he or she perceives and values the students in the school. Many adults are not always aware of the attitudes they have, yet these perceptions greatly affect our ability to be asset builders.

## HOW TO USE THIS HANDOUT

During a staff meeting, facilitate the following activity and follow up with the activity described on the handout.

Organize staff in groups of four and do the following:

1. Ask each group to choose some simple object in the room (notebook, pen, chair, marker, paper clip, etc).

2. Ask each group to list the positive features of the object and how it might be useful. Encourage them to think of atypical uses—for example, the chair can be broken into pieces to make a warming fire or to build a lobster trap.

3. Have each group share its object and uses.

4. Compare the exercise of finding value in everyday objects with finding value in our students. What would happen if we only considered the limitations of the objects? Of the students?

5. Discuss ways in which, as asset builders, we must look for and reinforce positive characteristics in the students we interact with.

6. Use the student lesson scenarios to teach the difference between viewing students in terms of limitations and viewing them with asset building in mind. Ask staff to separate into small groups, discuss the scenarios, fill in the handout, and report what they learned to the larger group.

# NEW PERCEPTIONS

*Think about the following situations and how you can view the students with a new perspective.*

| SCENARIO | STUDENT'S STRENGTHS | HOW THESE STRENGTHS CAN HELP THE STUDENT |
|---|---|---|
| Jon talks out loud in the classroom whenever he feels like it. When asked to stop, he does so only temporarily. Student snickering and laughter at his antics seem to spur him on. After multiple confrontations, Jon becomes disrespectful toward the teacher and to other students who try to quiet him. | | |
| Nessa frequently causes disruption in the cafeteria. Each day it's something different—cutting in front of others in line, telling students to move from "her" table, complaining about the food to the food servers. She usually has a large group of girls surrounding her; her bold personality demands attention. Efforts to rein Nessa in and get her to show respect for others make little impact. She lets cafeteria monitors know that she doesn't like rules and doesn't want to be told what to do. | | |

45

**45**

| SCENARIO | STUDENT'S STRENGTHS | HOW THESE STRENGTHS CAN HELP THE STUDENT |
|---|---|---|
| Mario is late for school almost every day. Detention makes no difference because he's dependent on adults in his household to give him a ride to school and he can't control when they'll get him there. Mario is smart but his grades are poor. He spends most of his time in class reading comic books and sketching in his notepad that he always seems to have with him. | | |
| Latosha is constantly being brought to the office for skipping classes. She's usually found in the girls' locker room, reading mystery novels. She doesn't relate to her classmates, but spends quite a bit of time talking to the custodian about mystery books. | | |

# WHO HELPED ME?

**KEY USER/S**
All school staff

**ASSET CATEGORY**
Support, Empowerment,
Boundaries and Expectations

**ASSETS ADDRESSED**
#3, Other Adult Relationships
#7, Community Values Youth
#14, Adult Role Models

46

## KEEP THIS IN MIND

Most of us have had at least one adult in our lives
who deeply affected us in a good way. Sometimes
it's tempting to tell ourselves that others are better asset builders than we are. But if you take a
few minutes to think about the adults who were
important for you when you were growing up,
you'll realize that many were "just folks"—the
neighbor next door, a friend's mom or dad, the
guy who umpired all your summer ball games.
It just takes a few of these memories to realize
that all of us have the ability—and the responsibility—to help young people build assets.

## HOW TO USE THIS HANDOUT

Think about it. Which adult made a deep im-
pression on you? Was there someone in your life
who made you feel good about who you were
when you were young? Who was it? What was

it they did? Use the following handout to help
fellow staff members visualize how they might
build assets with and for students in your school.
This handout can be used briefly during a staff
meeting as an icebreaker/meeting closer, or you
can devote an hour to the topic, inviting staff to
pair off or separate into small groups and discuss
who was there for them as a young person. You
might also watch the video *You Have to Live It,*
available from Search Institute.

## NOTES:

**46**

# WHO HELPED ME?

1. Name an adult in your childhood or adolescence who had a deep and positive influence on you.

2. What specifically did that person do to help you?

3. What attitude did that person have toward you? Did you have a sense that this person respected you or trusted you or held you in high regard?

4. How did that person show he or she valued you? Be specific.

5. They were unintentionally building which asset?

6. Knowing how deeply these actions or attitudes affected you when you were young, how can you show students that you value them?

# EMPHASIZE THE POSITIVE

**KEY USER/S**
All school staff

**ASSET CATEGORY**
Support, Empowerment

**ASSETS ADDRESSED**
#5, Caring School Climate
#7, Community Values Youth

## KEEP THIS IN MIND

The beauty of asset building is that anyone can do it anytime. We can all be asset builders by making a conscious shift in how we perceive students and how we talk to them. The key to being an asset builder is simple—all we have to do is see and respond to what is right with young people. Seeing what is right with students means feeling and showing that we are confident that they can achieve and succeed and that they are capable of engaging in positive behavior. Our attitude toward students is telling: young people know in an instant what adults really think. The quality and tenor of individual relationships with students and the general school environment convey a great deal to students about how the adults in their world at school regard and value them.

## HOW TO USE THIS HANDOUT

Use this handout to inspire staff members to build assets intentionally every day. The first list can help adults shift their focus and look at young people with a more positive perspective. The second list offers adults basic ideas for interacting with students in a way that is positive, warm, and caring. This handout is also a great follow-up to Activity Handout 46, "Who Helped Me?" Invite individuals to post these simple ideas in their classroom, staff lounge, or cafeteria.

## NOTES:

# EMPHASIZE THE POSITIVE

## POSITIVE THOUGHTS

- Young people have strengths that can be used to overcome deficits and problems.

- Having high expectations for students tells them I value them and see great promise in their abilities.

- My power as a teacher comes from the relationships I develop with my students.

- I am a powerful asset builder in the lives of my students.

- Asset building is important because it shows a commitment to the well-being of young people.

## POSITIVE INTERACTIONS

- Learn students' names and use them in all interactions.

- Greet students warmly and be sure to make eye contact.

- Focus daily on students' gifts and talents.

- Expand your positive influence by developing relationships with students you don't know yet.

- As often as possible, do something for a student that goes beyond her or his normal expectations.

- Encourage students to perform at higher levels and reward them when they do.

- Take time to listen.

- Take the initiative to meet and greet students and engage them in positive ways. Stand out in the hallways, circulate at lunch, and be available between or after classes.

# IN THE PRINCIPAL'S OFFICE

# FEED THE STAFF

**KEY USER/S**
Principals, school admin-
istrators

**ASSET CATEGORY**
Support

**ASSETS ADDRESSED**
#5, Caring School Climate

**48**

**NOTES:**

## KEEP THIS IN MIND

There's an old warning that says, "If you don't feed the staff, they'll eat the children." School principals and administrators can nurture top-down asset building. How? Build staff assets. Identify and report staff strengths. Reward as-set-building activities. Look for opportunities for staff to take time for staff development or other special activities that promote their own assets and those of the students they connect with every day.

## HOW TO USE THIS HANDOUT

Use the ideas in the handout to "feed the staff." Be a strong advocate for staff by helping them find the time to learn about asset building and develop skills needed to build assets for and with students. Post the handout in the staff lounge, office, or lunchroom.

# FEED THE STAFF

- During staff meetings and staff retreats, start a "Kudos to the Staff" or "Staff of the Day" ritual. Use that ritual to identify and reward asset builders among staff members. Include all school staff in the kudos program, including food services workers, custodians, bus drivers, and office staff.

- Use tributes to staff members to explain in detail how that person helped to build assets for students. Sharing specific details will give other staff members ideas about ways they too can become asset builders.

- Regular staff meetings can also become a forum for featuring an asset of the month. Ask staff to choose an asset they would like to emphasize for the next few weeks. Post the asset in the faculty lounge, ask for feedback throughout the month, and share ideas about ways to promote the selected asset.

- Know all the staff members in your school community. That includes every adult who interacts with students in the school. Connect with parent and other adult volunteers, security staff, and students.

48

# STUDENTS AS NATURAL RESOURCES

**KEY USER/S**
Principals, school administrators

**ASSET CATEGORY**
Support, Empowerment

**ASSETS ADDRESSED**
#5, Caring School Climate
#8, Youth as Resources

**49**

## KEEP THIS IN MIND

The culture of the school is influenced by the beliefs and actions of the principal and the administrative team. So it's important for them to model treating students as valuable resources within the school. Principals and administrative staff can engage all students in major decisions about the quality of their school life.

## HOW TO USE THIS HANDOUT

Many decisions crop up daily that in some way affect the quality of school life for students. Principals and administrative staff can use the tips in the handout to engage students in decision making and find opportunities to ask young people to lead. This handout can be distributed to the student body and then collected and reviewed by administrative staff members. As a follow-up, young people could be invited to a special meeting to talk about improving the school community.

Here some ways to see students as natural resources:

- Top priority! Know all students' names and know something about them.
- Take time to talk with students often and really listen to what they have to say.
- Handle student complaints by asking them to generate solutions.
- Create ways for students to communicate directly with school administration (e.g., open-door day, suggestion box, student-administration forums).
- Use student talents, skills, and resourcefulness to effect change—let students know you view them as agents for change.
- Give students responsibility and authority whenever possible.
- Develop and advertise specific processes through which students can voice and make changes.
- Empower students to monitor each other by giving them responsible roles.
- Model valuing students as resources for teachers and other school staff.
- Offer public recognition or rewards for student governance activities.
- Look for opportunities to give students power—and the responsibility that entails—whenever possible.

# YOU MAKE THE DIFFERENCE!

WE WANT TO MAKE OUR SCHOOL A PLACE WHERE EVERYONE FEELS WELCOME, BUT WE NEED YOUR HELP. PLEASE FILL OUT THIS FORM AND TURN IT IN TO THE SCHOOL OFFICE.

What are the things that you're concerned about at our school?

Who are some of the students whom you consider leaders?

How can young people feel more encouraged to take on leadership roles in the school? What should those roles look like (such as student government or a youth advisory board)? How can we ensure that everyone who wants to is encouraged to and has the chance to participate?

Write or draw your ideas here:

**49**

# POSITIVE PAPER TRAIL

**50**

**KEY USER/S**
School principals, administrators

**ASSET CATEGORY**
All

**ASSETS ADDRESSED**
All

## KEEP THIS IN MIND

Schools are notorious for being awash in paper—forms, mission statements, IEP plans, school reports, strategic plans, notes to home, etc. As long as the paper is being printed and distributed, why not add asset-building language to the information stream?

## HOW TO USE THIS HANDOUT

Use the handout to stimulate ideas about the printed material that is used, copied, and distributed throughout the school. Add simple phrases or sentences, asset logos, and/or asset language to all school communications.

## EXAMPLE:

Asset logos can be developed by students and applied to school products and uniforms—anything that usually carries the school logo. Add phrases like "Students who read succeed!" or "Celebrate (School Name)'s Students!" or "Students are our best asset."

## NOTES:

# POSITIVE PAPER TRAIL

Our school can be a better place to build assets by creating a positive paper trail. Consider adding asset language to these existing materials and communications that already routinely reach people within the school community.

- School publications: newsletter, student paper, school calendar, and yearbook
- School signage: cafeteria, bulletin boards, banners, and special events
- School Web site
- Cable access channel programming
- School and individual voice mail messages
- Office forms: fax, letterhead, notepads, and other forms
- Reports: parent organizations, strategic plans, mission statements
- School uniforms: jerseys, water bottles, anything that has the school logo
- Home forms: field trip authorizations, medical forms, and other home communications

We pledge to take the following steps to promote asset building in our school community:

1.

2.

3.

Here is how we will accomplish it:

We hope to have completed this by:

**50**

# SUSPENDING SUSPENSION

**KEY USER/S**
Principals, assistant principals, guidance counselors, and social workers

**ASSET CATEGORY**
Support, Boundaries and Expectations, Commitment to Learning, Positive Values

**ASSETS ADDRESSED**
#5, Caring School Climate
#12, School Boundaries
#22, School Engagement
#30, Responsibility

## KEEP THIS IN MIND

Student behavior that warrants suspension implies the inherent need to build assets in the life of that young person. These students need help to identify the positives in their lives and strengthen their connection to the school community. Principals and other school staff involved with suspended students can view each suspension as an opportunity for one-on-one asset-building work.

## HOW TO USE THIS HANDOUT

The activity handout offers tips to help principals and other school staff accomplish two essential asset-building goals with students facing suspension: identify and enhance the positives and deepen ties to the school.

**NOTES:**

# SUSPENDING SUSPENSION

School staff can use the following tips as asset-building tools to help students facing suspension.

## ENHANCE THE POSITIVES

- Pair students with a teacher/mentor whom they like and respect
- Ask students to name their favorite staff member and connect them in a specific activity, possibly over the course of a semester. Ask the staff member to periodically report on the student's progress.
- Ask one or more staff members to be a visible or invisible mentor for students.
- Find out what students are good at—what talents, special interests, or skills they have. Match these talents and strengths with a specific activity that gives students a chance to shine.
- Ask students to use a strength they have to help another student.
- Have students write a script, create a song, make a video, or use the means of their choice to answer the question, *Can one young person make a difference?*
- Put students in charge. Find an activity they can be responsible for, give them reasonable boundaries and expectations, and follow up to see that the job was completed.

## STRENGTHEN SCHOOL BONDS

- Create a discipline committee and invite students who have been suspended to serve on the committee. The group can be charged with learning about the developmental assets framework and identifying and publishing behavior that warrants suspension, along with asset-building ways to replace negative behavior with positive.
- Add participation in a "students empowered" group to the suspension consequences. Group activities and goals might include creating a poster with a checklist of behavior that warrants suspension paired with behavior that reflects asset building; creation of a short drama to be acted out during an all-school assembly; discussions about better ways to handle problems; and participation in organized service projects.
- Find social service or school service activities for students to do during suspension days, rather than sending them home. Make sure they're involved in activities that serve others and focus on the welfare or problems of others.
- Be creative with suspension consequences. Instead of days spent off school grounds, require students to serve within the school's boundaries. Create a list of activities that engage the students in the life of the school or connect them with a caring school staff member. Activities might include acting as assistant coach on one of the sports teams; serving as stage or prop manager for plays; working with art teachers to research an art topic that will be presented in the classroom; participating on a school activities planning committee; participating in student council meetings; or writing a column in the school newspaper.
- Expect successful participation in anger, stress, and/or time management groups.

**51**

# ON THE SCHOOL BUS

# RULES OF THE ROAD

**KEY USER/S**
School bus drivers

**ASSET CATEGORY**
Support, Boundaries and Expectations

**ASSETS ADDRESSED**
#3, Other Adult Relationships
#5, Caring School Climate
#12, School Boundaries
#14, Adult Role Models

## KEEP THIS IN MIND

School bus drivers are the first people outside of the family to see and greet students each day. Just a smile and personal greeting can be enough to re-adjust the social or emotional barometer for young people. Bus drivers are also the last school staff members students see each day. In that capacity, drivers can make a bad day better and leave a student looking forward to tomorrow—if nothing else, just for the warm greeting and the ride to school the next morning.

## HOW TO USE THIS HANDOUT

The handout is designed as a minposter that provides tips for building relationships and a list of questions that will help students generate their own rules for bus behavior. These questions are based on assets. Encourage bus drivers to carry these ideas with them and post them on their buses.

## NOTES:

52

# RULES OF THE ROAD

Drivers can set clear boundaries and have high expectations for students. They can catch students doing something well. They can make the students responsible for creating the rules of bus etiquette and the consequences for breaking those rules. Drivers can make sitting in the front of the bus an honor rather than a discipline. Here's a real-life example:

## Driving Home Assets

While it may be technically accurate to say that what Mary Yagel did for 31 years was drive a big, yellow school bus in suburban Rochester, New York, that factual statement misses the heart and soul of what she was up to. Yagel, who has since retired, made it her business to be a positive daily presence in the lives of the children who rode her bus. "If you're firm, friendly, and fair and have that consistently," Yagel says, "you develop a bond." Here are some of the ways Yagel built assets:

**LEARNING THE NAMES** of all the students who rode her bus.

**ENCOURAGING LEADERSHIP IN THE OLDER STUDENTS.** "If there was a problem on the bus, I'd look up in my mirror and have eye-to-eye contact with the older kids. Then they'd go and whisper in the student's ear, 'You need to sit down.'"

**ATTENDING SCHOOL FUNCTIONS AND SPORTS EVENTS.** "For some kids, there's nobody there for them. But they knew me. They saw me every day and saw that I was there for them."

Information adapted from "Portrait of an asset builder: Mary Yagel drives home assets." Found in *Assets: The Magazine of Ideas for Healthy Communities and Healthy Youth,* Autumn 1999.

**52**

### Here's how you can connect!

- Learn and use each student's name.
- Learn something about each student who rides the bus.
- Say hello and good bye to students and make eye contact when addressing them.
- Listen to students and respond to them.
- Do something with or for students outside of your routine.
- Stay in touch and maintain contact when possible.

### Rules of the Road

- What behavior do we need on the bus?
- How can we reward the good stuff? How can we show appreciation to those who make the ride better?
- What are some things each of us can do to make a better ride each day?
- What should the driver do when behavior is out of line?
- Should the driver be the only one who enforces the rules? Who else can/should do it?

**52**

# FIRST DAY FUN

**KEY USER/S**
School bus drivers

**ASSET CATEGORY**
Support, Constructive
Use of Time

**ASSETS ADDRESSED**
#5, Caring School Climate
#17, Creative Activities

## HOW TO USE THIS HANDOUT

Bus drivers can use this handout to create a card featuring a snapshot of each student to send home to parents and guardians. Students can even fill in some parts of the card when they take it home and talk with their parents or guardians about their first day of school.

## KEEP THIS IN MIND

School bus drivers don't always have a lot of time to interact with students or to really get to know the students' names. Mary Yagel, a retired bus driver from Rochester, New York, found a great way to build relationships with students and connect with parents. She decided to take photos of students on their first day of school and send the snapshots home to busy parents and guardians. Yagel started this practice after noticing that more and more working parents and guardians were unable to see their children off on this special day. "I'd make a personal card from the photo and put their name and the school and the year on it. If there were double prints, then I'd make sure the grandparents also got one."

## NOTES:

**53**

Information adapted from, "Portrait of an asset builder: Mary Yagel drives home assets." Found in *Assets: The Magazine of Ideas for Healthy Communities and Healthy Youth,* Autumn 1999.

# FIRST DAY FUN

Dear _____,

*(Insert date)*_____ was your child's first day of school and I thought you might like to see what they looked like on our school bus. Take a moment and fill out the bottom portion together with your child.  Here's to a wonderful new year!

> Place Photo Here

**53**

My name is _____ and I am _____ years  old.

My bus driver's name is _____ and my

teacher's name is _____.

I live at this address _____

_____

# IN THE NURSE'S OFFICE

# TEACHING HEALTHY HABITS

**KEY USER/S**
School nurses

**ASSET CATEGORY**
Support, Positive Values

**ASSETS ADDRESSED**
#3, Other Adult Relationships
#5, Caring School Climate
#30, Responsibility

## KEEP THIS IN MIND

School nurses are not just in the business of sticking on bandages. They have a great opportunity to practice preventive medicine by talking with students, gaining their trust, and then teaching them about things like good nutrition, personal hygiene, and immunizations. If nurses can establish trust with older students, they can talk with them about risky behaviors such as smoking, alcohol and other drug use, sexual activity, and eating disorders. Nurses can also talk to students who have special health-care needs, such as diabetes or epilepsy, about how to manage their health. It all starts with a simple conversation.

## HOW TO USE THIS HANDOUT

Think of the handout as a conversation starter. The goal is, first, to engage students in conversation—get them talking about anything. The next step is to establish trust so that students become willing to discuss health-related topics and are open to hearing the advice and information nurses can share.

## NOTES:

54

# TEACHING HEALTHY HABITS

## CONVERSATION STARTERS

Use this list of talking points and open-ended questions to encourage friendly conversation with the students who come to the nurse's office for various complaints and ailments:

- What is your favorite subject in school? Why?

- What subject do you like least? Why?

- What do you like to do for fun?

- Do you have brothers or sisters? Are any of them at the school?

- Who are your best friends at school? Why do you like them? What is it about each that you enjoy?

- Who is your favorite teacher or coach? What is it that you like about that person?

- Are you involved in any special activities at school? clubs? sports? drama?

- Do you have any questions or concerns about your health? Do you feel like you're in good health?

- Do you smoke? Does anyone in your family smoke at home?

- What are your eating habits like?

- How often do you miss school because you're sick?

**54**

# YOU'RE BUILDING A HEALTHY SCHOOL!

**KEY USER/S**
School nurses

**ASSET CATEGORY**
Support

**ASSETS ADDRESSED**
#1, Family Support
#3, Other Adult Relationships
#5, Caring School Climate

**NOTES:**

## KEEP THIS IN MIND

School nurses can build healthy bodies and healthy spirits. Usually students are sent to the school nurse when something is wrong—sickness, broken bones, bruises. It's a comfort to see a caring face that is concerned about their well-being. Nurses can take that goodwill a step further and reinforce the positive behavior they see on an average school day.

## HOW TO USE THIS HANDOUT

The following handout can be filled out by the school nurse and given to students who have been spotted doing something that makes the school a healthier place for everyone (e.g., helping a younger student, refusing to follow the lead of a class bully, offering her or his assistance to a school secretary or teacher without being asked).

# YOU'RE BUILDING A HEALTHY SCHOOL!

Hi, _____

*(student's name)*

You did something really great today! ☺ Here's what I saw:

I am very proud of you.

Thank you,

Staff person's name _____    Date _____

55

# IN THE GUIDANCE OFFICE

# ASSET BUILDING FOR BULLIES AND VICTIMS

**KEY USER/S**
All school staff

**ASSET CATEGORY**
Support, Social Competencies

**ASSETS ADDRESSED**
#5, Caring School Climate
#33, Interpersonal Competence
#36, Peaceful Conflict Resolution

## KEEP THIS IN MIND

In every incident of bullying, two students are harmed—the victim as well as the bully. Each needs help building assets that will make her or him less likely to bully or be bullied. Anyone in the schoo l community who witnesses bullying can be an asset builder, including students.

## HOW TO USE THIS HANDOUT

The handout offers a series of steps to take to prevent bullying before it happens and deal with it when it does take place. Some of these steps aid schools in prevention, some help identify bullies and victims, and some help students develop needed assets.

**NOTES:**

# ASSET BUILDING FOR BULLIES AND VICTIMS

*1. Educate yourself about the problem.*

Learn about bullying by checking out printed materials or going to Internet sites like the following and type "bullying" in the search engines:

- www.partnershipforlearning.org (Partnership for Learning)
- www.cfchildren.org (Committee for Children)
- www.nwrel.org (Northwest Regional Educational Laboratory)
- www.education-world.com (Education World)

These are just a few of many resources available on the Internet, but sites change often, so do some surfing!

*2. Recognize the problem.*

- Build awareness among teachers and all other school staff who interact with students to know what bullying behavior is.
- Teach students to recognize the traits of bullies and victims.

*3. Respond immediately.*

- Respond quickly and effectively.
- Know your own style of resolving conflicts, discuss it with other school staff members, and define a schoolwide approach to conflict resolution.

- Help students develop understanding and empathy for victims. Help students think of ways to help bullies and victims build assets that make them less likely to bully or be bullied.
- Talk with parents of both bullies and victims and engage them in asset-building brainstorming and activities.

*4. Develop assets.*

- For victims, focus on building assets that enhance confidence, help in making friends, and minimize isolation. Encourage activities that get these students engaged and connected.
- For bullies, work on building self-esteem and social skills along with healthy conflict resolution techniques. Modeling appropriate conflict resolution and problem-solving skills is also a good way to help.

**56**

# ACCENT WHAT'S RIGHT WITH STUDENTS

**KEY USER/S**
Guidance counselors, social workers, prevention specialists

**ASSET CATEGORY**
Support, Empowerment

**ASSETS ADDRESSED**
#3, Other Adult Relationships
#5, Caring School Climate
#10, Safety

## KEEP THIS IN MIND

School counselors, social workers, and prevention specialists have the chance to make a difference in the lives of "extra-ordinary" students. These are the students who have something out of the ordinary happening that calls for special attention. School systems and even state mandates often require that we identify what is wrong with the student. The asset-building approach asks that we also learn what is right. And further, asset builders push aside the temptation to deal only with the situation at hand. Instead, they take time to learn about and fully appreciate the whole child, not just the presenting problem that demands the most immediate attention.

## HOW TO USE THIS HANDOUT

When working with students, the typical conversation starts with the problem at hand and follows this pattern: What happened? Why did it happen? What was your role in the situation? What was inappropriate about your actions? What are possible solutions to the problem so it doesn't happen again? What consequences should be applied? Use the checklist in the following handout to have a different kind of exchange with the student. The checklist will help you engage in an alternative, asset-building conversation that leaves the student with ego intact, perhaps a better sense of her or his strengths, and a positive adult connection.

## NOTES:

**57**

# ACCENT WHAT'S RIGHT WITH STUDENTS

### BE INTENTIONALLY INVITING.
Introduce yourself to the student, use the student's name or nickname, make eye contact, and be open and warm.

### CONNECT AND CONVERSE.
Have a meaningful conversation. Listen for help identifying the student's strengths and passions.

### ACCEPT AND AFFIRM.
Use your knowledge of youth development to encourage optimism and authenticity in students.

### OFFER ADVICE.
Share experience that will help the student shape reality.

### RECEIVE ADVICE.
Young people have exquisite wisdom.

### EXPRESS CARE.
Follow up in person, write a note, do something with the student outside your routine.

### KEEP YOUR PROMISES.
Hold up your end of the bargain and expect the student to honor her or his commitments.

### BUILD SAFETY.
Students who feel safe and valued will stay connected.

### ENGAGE IN PARTNERSHIP.
Help students view their participation and contributions as helpful.

### SHARE CONTROL.
Allow students to lead.

### ACKNOWLEDGE THE POSITIVE.
Name and reward positive behavior.

*Contributed by Marilyn Peplau, Search Institute trainer and consultant for Vision Training Associates.*

**57**

# TALENT SEARCH

**KEY USER/S**
Guidance counselors, social workers

**ASSET CATEGORY**
Positive Identity

**ASSETS ADDRESSED**
#40, Positive View of Personal Future

## KEEP THIS IN MIND

It's critical for those involved in school support services to avoid gloomy predictions for a student's future. Instead, guidance counselors and social workers must develop the knack for discovering students' talents and strengths. What do they like to do? What are they good at? What are their aspirations and hopes? When they look ahead to the future, what do they wish for themselves?

## HOW TO USE THIS HANDOUT

Work with students in groups or individually to conduct a talent search. Use the handout to spur discussion about the future and to find out if students are optimistic about where they can and will go in life. Distribute the handout, have students fill it out (without putting their names on it), and turn it in. Mix up the handouts and re-distribute them. Ask students to read their handouts out loud as though they are theirs—ask them to play the role of the handout author.

Have the other students ask questions and discuss the handout responses. The student who is the real owner of the handout responses will get an interesting reality check and perhaps a revised sense of her or his talents!

## NOTES:

**58**

# TALENT SEARCH

## 1. MY SPECIAL TALENTS INCLUDE:

__ Being a good listener       __ Being organized       __ Speaking more than one language

__ Good at speaking in public   __ Being able to sing   __ Being a good dancer

Other_____

## 2. HERE ARE THE THINGS I'M REALLY GOOD AT:

__ Music        __ Drawing       __ Cooking

__ Sports       __ Computers     __ Math

__ Poetry       __ Spelling      __ Making people laugh

Other_____

## 3. IN THE FUTURE, I'D LIKE TO:

___ Visit a different country        ____ Become an Olympic athlete

___ Become an artist                 ____ Become a parent

___ Go to college                    ____ Change the world by_____

Other _____

58

PASS IT ON **AT SCHOOL!** ——————————————————

**Activity Handout 58**

**4. TO GET TO WHERE I WANT TO GO, I NEED TO DEVELOP THESE SKILLS OR TALENTS:**

**5. HERE'S HOW I CAN START DEVELOPING THOSE TALENTS.** (ASK THE OTHER STUDENTS FOR IDEAS!)

**58**

# SKILLS FOR LIFE

**KEY USER/S**
Prevention specialists

**ASSET CATEGORY**
Social Competencies

**ASSETS ADDRESSED**
#35, Resistance Skills
#36, Peaceful Conflict
Resolution

**NOTES:**

## KEEP THIS IN MIND

To be most effective, prevention specialists must work with many parts of the school community—students, teachers, student support staff, and parents. The asset framework blends with what the work prevention specialists are already doing by encouraging all the members of the school community to interact with one another to support the positive development of every student. When students have more assets, they are likely to be more successful.

## HOW TO USE THIS HANDOUT

Prevention specialists can use the handout as a checklist for helping students build assets. Such efforts should take place on several levels within the school community. The checklist will serve as a reminder to address all of them.

# SKILLS FOR LIFE

## PREVENTION SPECIALIST CHECKLIST—BUILDING SKILLS FOR LIFE

❑ Work directly with students to help them build assets.

❑ Work within student assistance programs to focus interventions on what's right and healthy as well as what's wrong or risky.

❑ Educate the larger school community to promote programs and awareness building based on an asset-building framework.

❑ Work with student support staff (counselors, social workers, and home-school liaisons) to coach them in how to become asset builders.

❑ Promote programs to teach conflict resolution and refusal skills to students—a way to build assets that translate into important life skills.

❑ Screen potential programs, practices, and expenditures—do they intentionally contribute to students' assets?

**59**

# WORK AND LEARN

**KEY USER/S**
Schoolwide initiative

**ASSET CATEGORY**
Boundaries and Expectations, Commitment to Learning, Positive Identity

**ASSETS ADDRESSED**
#14, Adult Role Models
#22, School Engagement
#39, Sense of Purpose

## KEEP THIS IN MIND

Schools must find ways to connect with disengaged students. One way to do this is to develop a mentor/work-skills program that connects students with school office, custodial, or other staff. For example, students working in the office can be intentionally exposed to a variety of clerical skills and procedures. Students working with custodial staff can be introduced to the roles, responsibilities, and skills of a building manager. The bonus is the time students spend with a school adult.

## HOW TO USE THIS HANDOUT

The handout includes ideas for ways to involve students in the day-to-day school operation. Students should be connected with a caring adult who is willing to supervise the student. The school staff member should be prepared to

structure the learning experience. The student needs to know what is expected and how to perform the work (operate copier, answer phones, greet visitors to the school, order supplies, etc.). The adult should monitor daily, offer help and praise, and periodically meet with the student to review performance and alter responsibilities to keep the work interesting.

## NOTES:

**60**

# WORK AND LEARN

School isn't just a place for students to spend their time reading and learning from books. It's also a place where they can begin to gain skills that can prepare them for the future.

Here are some ideas for how to focus on the talents and gifts of young people in classrooms, after-school programs, and detention.

| Student's gift | Where the student would work: | What the student would be doing | What the student would gain: |
|---|---|---|---|
| **Does the student work well independently?** | School office | Keyboarding/typing, copying, answering phones, greeting visitors, filing | Experience working with various computer programs and other office equipment, direct contact with school staff |
| **Does the student like to work with her or his hands?** | Custodian/sanitation team | Basic maintenance, supply ordering, basic repair | Practical training |
| **Is he or she a good cook?** | Cafeteria | Supply ordering, menu and food preparation, sanitation | Opportunity to serve students and create a menu that they like |
| **Is the student a good leader?** | After-school program | Recreation planning, homework help, supervision | Relationship building with staff and students |
| **Does he or she like sports?** | Assistant coach, equipment handling | Team management, practice and play strategy | A fun way to build skills and be a valuable part of the team |

**60**

# BALANCING STEPS

**KEY USER/S**
Challenging youth

**ASSET CATEGORY**
Support, Empowerment, Boundaries and
Expectations

**ASSETS ADDRESSED**
#3, Other Adult Relationships
#5, Caring School Climate
#9, Service to Others
#12, School Boundaries
#16, High Expectations

## KEEP THIS IN MIND

Almost everyone likes to feel that he or she
has something to offer. School communities can
help even the most challenging students find
success by tapping into their altruism. Many challenging students fight feelings of isolation, lone-
liness, or being marginalized. Counter this by
helping these students develop a bond with the
school, even if that connection is small at first.
Connected students feel their sense of purpose
and in many instances are much more willing
and able to participate—in a good way—in the
life of the school.

Here are some ways staff can begin:

**OFFER YOUR TIME AND CARE.** Take the initiative to reach out to the student. Clearly tell
the student you want to talk to her or him
and will be available at any time. Set up a
specific time for a first contact.

**MAKE TIME AND CREATE SPACE.** Be available
or structure times to talk. Make sure there's
a private place to talk. Repeat that you will always be available whenever the student needs
to be with someone or to talk.

**FOCUS ON STRENGTHS.** Spend little time on
discussion of problems and much time on
drawing out strengths.

**CREATE SAFE PLACES.** Work with the student
to identify emotionally and physically safe
places. Which adults are trustworthy? Where
is a safe living arrangement?

**HELP WITH SETTING GOALS.** Challenge the
student to set one goal and think through
how to reach that goal and when. Continue
to set goals, one at a time, and celebrate every
single success, small or large.

**SET AND COMMUNICATE CLEAR BOUNDARIES.**
Lay out some clear expectations for your relationship; this will show the student that you
believe in her or him.

**61**

CREATE OPPORTUNITIES. Find ways for the student to make real contributions. That might include asking the student to tutor someone, be a buddy for a younger student, or do service work in the community. As soon as you detect a talent or interest, match that with a real need.

## HOW TO USE THIS HANDOUT

The following handout can be used to invite students to be a part of the school community and help make positive change on behalf of themselves and others. Such activities might include a schoolwide cleanup project, offering a series of forums for students and staff to voice their opinions about the school's environment, or building a connection with a local business to offer students valuable work experience. Staff should be encouraged to identify a variety of students, not just the known leaders, to participate in such an activity. Students can be encouraged to attend by offering extra credit points for a social studies class or service-learning hours. Pizza parties and other fun activities are also a great way to bring students on board.

**NOTES:**

**61**

# BALANCING STEPS
## YOU'RE INVITED TO MAKE A DIFFERENCE IN OUR SCHOOL!

Dear _____,

I've noticed how important you are to our school community.

Here are some of the qualities I see in you:

The school is looking for more students like you to help us with . . .
(Organizer/coordinator fills this area in.)

Would you be willing to help us?

Take some time to think about this and then feel free to come and talk with me!

We are planning to have a meeting on _____

at_____.

## THANK YOU!

61

# DETENTION ATTENTION

**KEY USER/S**
Guidance counselors, school staff
who monitor detention

**ASSET CATEGORY**
Empowerment, Constructive Use
of Time, Positive Values

**ASSETS ADDRESSED**
#9, Service to Others
#18, Youth Programs
#26, Caring
#27, Equality and Social Justice

## KEEP THIS IN MIND

The main tool many schools use to create consequences for negative behavior is detention. If
each student in your school puts in one hour of
detention each school year and you have 1,000
students in the school, you have 1,000 hours of
student time that could be put to positive, asset-
building use.

## HOW TO USE THIS HANDOUT

The handout includes tips for using detention as
a way to empower students and perhaps create
positive waves in the school or community.

## NOTES:

**62**

# DETENTION ATTENTION

Tips for turning attention in detention to good use:

- Meet with other school staff who monitor detention to choose a service project that will allow detention monitors to involve students in a piecemeal kind of way. That is, because you'll be seeing students for just an hour and at infrequent intervals, find a service project that students can contribute to in the detention classroom for the hour you have them. For example, they could stuff envelopes for a local food bank fund-raiser.

- Involve students you see only occasionally in detention in a service project. Ask them to consider volunteering additional time by coming back to the detention room to help whenever they have extra time.

- Involve "repeaters" in a more engaging way in the service project. Put them in charge of some daily task. For example, put a student in charge of a small group of students who need to stuff 100 envelopes by the end of the detention hour.

- Make a "Detention Attention" suggestion box, place it in the office or staff lounge, and ask school staff to write requests for small, short tasks they need help with. What can 20 or 30 students accomplish in one hour? Quite a lot! Engage students in activities that really need doing and find a way to thank them later for their participation. Let them know how what they did helped.

- Put students in charge of their own time by asking them to state at the beginning of detention what they will accomplish by the end of the hour. Don't dismiss them until they have demonstrated to the monitor that the task is finished.

- By midyear, gather a list of names of "repeaters" and, at a staff meeting, ask school staff to volunteer to be either a visible or invisible mentor for the student whose name they selected.

**62**

# EYES ON THE FUTURE

**KEY USER/S**
Guidance counselors

**ASSET CATEGORY**
Positive Identity

**ASSETS ADDRESSED**
#39, Sense of Purpose
#40, Positive View of Personal Future

## KEEP THIS IN MIND

Guidance counselors are frequently used for everything but guidance. Their role is often turned into that of hall monitors, disciplinarians, and cafeteria and detention supervisors. Let's put the "guide" back into the guidance counselor's role.

## HOW TO USE THIS HANDOUT

The handout is a questionnaire designed to help guidance counselors engage students in thinking about the future. Students who share similar interests can be grouped together to explore various options. Ask students to use the questions to reflect on their values, hopes, and sense of purpose in life. Encourage students to share their responses during small group discussion and then share some of what they've learned in a larger group. It will also be helpful to direct students to resources (books, Web sites, people) that can help them pinpoint their interests and determine what their future might look like. Follow-up is also a great way to keep students on the right track and support their goals.

## NOTES:

# EYES ON THE FUTURE

1.  What is **important** to you? When you're having a bad day, what **keeps you going**?

2.  When you think of the future are you hopeful? What do you **look forward to** most?

3.  How would you like **your life** to be in five years? in 10 years or 15 years?

4.  What are you **worried about** when you think about the future?

5.  What kinds of things do you think you need **help** with as you prepare for the future? (What would you like to learn? What kinds of people would you like to connect with?)

6.  What can **you do** today, tomorrow, or next week to connect to your future?

**63**

# IN THE LOCKER ROOM/ON THE FIELD

# RULES OF THE GAME

**KEY USER/S**
School staff, coaches

**ASSET CATEGORY**
Social Competencies

**ASSETS ADDRESSED**
#33, Interpersonal Competence

## KEEP THIS IN MIND

Team sports give coaches a great opportunity to help students learn that teams formed around bonds of friendship and empathy are teams that win in more places than on the field, court, or mat. By allowing young people of various skill levels to play on the same team, coaches can lead the way in teaching young people to play their best and respect the varying skills of their teammates. They can also help players get better at building the strength of the team instead of focusing on themselves.

## HOW TO USE THIS HANDOUT

During the first team meeting, use this handout to create a list (using a white board, blackboard, or newsprint) detailing how you want team members to treat each other. Such guidelines are always more effective when young people are encouraged to come up with the rules by and for themselves. Start with a blank slate—ask team members to explain how they want to see teammates behave toward each other and what consequences should follow when these rules are broken. Encourage the students to be creative with the consequences—for example, taking home all the jerseys and washing them for the team after a game or two, or being water boy or water girl during games. When finished, make copies and hand them out to team members to think about. Ask them to sign the guidelines to show their commitment to honoring them.

## HERE'S AN EXAMPLE OF WHAT A TEAM MIGHT COME UP WITH:

**TEAM RULE 1:** Respecting each other, even when we disagree

**CONSEQUENCE OF BREAKING THE RULE:** Public apology

- - - - - - - - - - - - - - - - - - - - - - - - - - - - - - - - - - - -

**TEAM RULE 2:** Being a team player

**CONSEQUENCE OF BREAKING THE RULE:** Sitting out a game and serving beverages and handing out towels

- - - - - - - - - - - - - - - - - - - - - - - - - - - - - - - - - - - -

**TEAM RULE 3:** Showing up to practice on time

**CONSEQUENCE OF BREAKING THE RULE:** Spending an equal amount of time after practice, assisting the coach and cleaning

- - - - - - - - - - - - - - - - - - - - - - - - - - - - - - - - - - - -

64

# RULES OF THE GAME

These are the things that we will commit to as members of this team :

| TEAM RULE 1 | CONSEQUENCE OF BREAKING THE RULE |
|---|---|
| TEAM RULE 2 | CONSEQUENCE OF BREAKING THE RULE |
| TEAM RULE 3 | CONSEQUENCE OF BREAKING THE RULE |
| TEAM RULE 4 | CONSEQUENCE OF BREAKING THE RULE |

I understand how I am expected to treat my teammates during the season of practices, games, and other team-related activities. I will do my part to support my team and help my teammates feel good about themselves and their efforts during the season.

Student's signature _____

**64**

# ANGER RISING: CONFLICT SOLUTIONS 101

**KEY USER/S**
School staff, coaches

**ASSET CATEGORY**
Social Competencies

**ASSETS ADDRESSED**
#36, Peaceful Conflict Resolution

## KEEP THIS IN MIND

Coaches can teach a profound lesson in peaceful conflict resolution by modeling those skills and not tolerating verbal abuse by parents and other adults on the sidelines. But let's be realistic. Players get mad at each other, at themselves, and at umpires and referees—even at their coaches! Coaches can help their players learn to resolve conflicts by teaching them some simple steps to take when conflicts arise.

## HOW TO USE THIS HANDOUT

Use a team meeting to ask players how they want to see conflicts resolved during the season. Use the examples on the handout to get them thinking about the kinds of conflicts that may arise. Write all their ideas on a white board. Give them the following handout, which outlines some basic steps for resolving conflicts. Ask the team to look at the steps for resolving conflicts on the handout and the ideas they came up with and decide what steps they, as a team, want to follow. Ask them to think of some consequences for teammates who don't use the conflict resolution steps and instead fly off the handle. Tell them to be creative in thinking up consequences. Make a large poster to put up in the locker room that reminds players of the steps and the consequences they agreed to.

## NOTES:

65

# ANGER RISING: CONFLICT SOLUTIONS 101

Everyone gets angry sometimes—at ourselves and at others. What might you get mad about during the course of a sports season? Try these scenarios for starters:

1. The coach reprimands you for showing up late for a practice, game, meet, or tournament.

2. Your teammate throws or sends you a lousy pass, you miss it, and you're the one who looks like a fool on the field.

3. The referee calls a penalty on you when in fact someone else did the nasty deed.

4. Your team loses because everyone is off that day. No one can do anything right, your teammates make mistakes, and you all look bad, even though you played a good, even great game.

5. Your friends tell you they'll be there to watch you play and don't show.

6. A parent on the sidelines yells at you for missing a pass or throw.

7. One of your teammates yells at you when you make a mistake.

When you feel the anger rising, follow these simple steps to solving the problem without turning up the heat.

*On your own:*

Step 1: Back off and count to ten. Remind yourself to take some deep breaths.

Step 2: If you're mad at someone else, talk to the person. Tell them how you feel about what happened and listen to their side. If you're mad at yourself, talk to someone else about your feelings.

Step 3: Suggest several ways to solve the problem.

Step 4: Choose one solution and act on it.

*With help from a third person:*

Step 1: Back off, count to ten, and ask for help from a coach or someone on your team who has volunteered to be the peace-keeper.

Step 2: Talk to the person; explain how you feel about what happened.

Step 3: Give the peacekeeper room to find out how the other person sees it—listen to what he or she says.

Step 4: Think of several solutions to the problem and choose one to act on.

**65**

These are some creative consequences for teammates (or myself) who lose it and don't use the conflict resolution steps. (Examples include teaching younger children about sportsmanship, assisting younger teams, and assisting the coaches of other teams.)


Creative consequence 1 _____


Creative consequence 2 _____


Creative consequence 3 _____

# GOOD PLAYERS ARE GOOD SPORTS

**KEY USER/S**
School staff, coaches

**ASSET CATEGORY**
Social Competencies

**ASSETS ADDRESSED**
#33, Interpersonal Competence

## KEEP THIS IN MIND

Coaches can help players succeed by setting expectations for good sportsmanship toward players on other teams, toward referees and umpires, and toward each other. Important ways for coaches to teach sportsmanship are modeling those skills, not tolerating verbal abuse by parents and other adults on the sidelines, and giving players a clear set of guidelines for good sportsmanship.

## HOW TO USE THIS HANDOUT

Ask players to volunteer to act out the roles described in the handout, beginning with Scene 1. Discuss what happens and engage youth in a discussion.

Ask such questions as:

1. What would a real team player do in a situation like this?

2. How can we ensure that we perform to the best of our ability and play fair?

3. How can we be good sports whether we win or lose?

Follow the same steps for the situation described in Scene 2. Create your own situation for Scene 3. During each discussion, write the traits of good sportsmanship, as defined by the players, on a board. Summarize the traits and create posters or team T-shirts with the traits written on them.

## NOTES:

# GOOD PLAYERS ARE GOOD SPORTS

## SCENE 1:
## ILLEGAL MOVE, BUT HEADING FOR THE WINNING GOAL

Cast needed: Player, opposing player, referee

Situation: It's the end of the game, the score is tied, and the crowd is screaming for a win. The ball is passed to the player, who catches it, turns, and rushes forward. The player pushes the opposing player aside as he or she moves down the field or court. The opposing player falls and is obviously hurt. The referee does not stop play, even though the opposing player is down. The player knows two things: first, the opposing player is hurt, and second, the player illegally tripped her or him. What does the player do?

## SCENE 2:
## PLAYING LIKE REAL WINNERS

Cast needed: One person to represent Team A, one person to represent Team B, Team A coach, and Team B coach.

Situation: The game is intense. The score has been tied over and over, first one team ahead and then the other. Team A has played a tough, dirty game. Team B has played a pretty clean game and has suffered some player injuries as a result of Team A's rough play. When the game ends, Team B loses by one lousy point. How does Team B handle the team lineup when they are expected to file by the Team A players and congratulate them? What does each coach tell the team about the win or loss?

## SCENE 3:

Cast needed:

Situation:

# RULES TO PLAY BY— FOR PARENTS ONLY

**KEY USER/S**
School staff, coaches

**ASSET CATEGORY**
Social Competencies

**ASSETS ADDRESSED**
#33, Interpersonal Competence
#36, Peaceful Conflict Resolution

## KEEP THIS IN MIND

Coaches can do a lot to help their players build skills in solving conflicts, respecting others, and being good sports. But what happens when unruly parents yell from the sidelines? And what happens if what they say conflicts with the coach's stated rules or expectations for behavior? The wrong thing to do is to allow such parents to be poor role models for the players. Coaches can launch a preventive strike against the bellowing sideline parent by giving players copies of "Rules for Behavior on the Sidelines" to take home for parents to read, sign, and return. Tell the team members they'll get their team uniforms as soon as they turn in their parent-signed copy!

## HOW TO USE THIS HANDOUT

Brainstorm with players what rules they would like people on the sidelines to abide by. Start the discussion by asking them, "What bugs you the most about things you hear from the sidelines while you're playing?" Give the players a few examples to get the discussion going: yelling instructions that conflict with what the coach has taught or is asking of the players, hearing negative things from the sidelines, parents yelling insults at referees or umpires. For each example, ask the players to make a corresponding rule. Keep track of the rules on a white board as discussion progresses. Create a handout that summarizes these rules or use the following handout and add other rules that players thought of. Then send it home for parents to sign and return.

## NOTES:

67

# RULES FOR BEHAVIOR ON THE SIDELINES

These are the rules for behavior on the sidelines that your child's team decided on:

1.  I will shout only positive, supportive encouragement from the sidelines for both teams.
2.  I will not try to tell players how to play or what they should be doing on field or on court—that's the coach's business and expertise.
3.  I will respect all decisions made by referees or umpires and will not shout out negative reactions when I disagree with a call.
4.  I will respect the coach's choice of starting lineup, substitutions, and other player decisions.
5.  I understand that every child deserves the chance to play, even when the score is close, even when there are other players on the team who can play better.
6.



7.



8.

(Please return the bottom portion)

- - - - - - - - - - - - - - - - - - - - - - - - - - - - - - - - - - - - - - - - - - - - - - - - - - - - - - - - - - - - - - - - - - -

I want to support my child and her or his successful participation on a team that plays for enjoyment and to build skills and does *not* play solely for winning. I agree to follow the rules for sideline behavior that my child's team has created.

**67**

Player's Name _____

*Parent's Signature* _____ Date _____

# IN PARENT MEETINGS

# YOU'RE THE EXPERTS

---

**KEY USER/S**
Parent leaders, parent organizations

**ASSET CATEGORY**
Support, Commitment to Learning

**ASSETS ADDRESSED**
#1, Family Support
#2, Positive Family Communication
#21, Achievement Motivation
#22, School Engagement
#23, Homework
#24, Bonding to School
#25, Reading for Pleasure

---

## KEEP THIS IN MIND

Parents know their children best. They are the experts when it comes to their children. Schools and teachers can tap into that knowledge and use it to strengthen students' assets by creating a regular, easy way for the voices of parents to be heard and their ideas honored.

## HOW TO USE THIS HANDOUT

The following handout will help to educate parents about the Commitment-to-Learning assets while giving them a way to tell teachers about their children. Before parent-teacher conferences, the handout can be mailed or sent home with students. You might also include a list of the developmental asset (Activity Handout 1). Ask parents to fill out the form and bring it with them to the parent-teacher conference. Discuss each item on the list with parents and ask them for ideas about how to strengthen each asset.

## NOTES:

# YOU'RE THE EXPERTS

## PARENT-TEACHER CONFERENCE CHECKLIST

Together we can strengthen your child's academic success by helping her or him develop a commitment to lifelong learning. Our school has decided to accomplish this goal by building the developmental assets with and for students. Developmental assets are the positive experiences and qualities all of us have the power to bring into the lives of children and youth. Please circle the phrase that best describes your child and bring this handout with you to the parent-teacher conference.

_____

(Your child's name)

1.  Wants to do well in school.

    Yes     Somewhat     No

    Comment:

2.  Is eager to learn.

    Yes     Somewhat     No

    Comment:

3.  Does at least one hour of homework every school day.

    Yes     Somewhat     No

    Comment:

4.  Cares about the school.

    Yes     Somewhat     No

    Comment:

5.  Reads for pleasure three or more hours per week.

    Yes     Somewhat     No

    Comment:

**68**

# PARENT POWER

**KEY USER/S**
Parents, guardians

**ASSET CATEGORY**
Support

**ASSETS ADDRESSED**
#1, Family Support
#2, Positive Family Communication
#6, Parent Involvement in Schooling

## KEEP THIS IN MIND

It's a fact. Parents are the single most important influence in the lives of students. Schools can strengthen the quality of the school community and climate for their students by connecting with parents or guardians.

## HOW TO USE THIS HANDOUT

Use the handout to give parents ideas about more and better ways to be involved in the lives of their children. Copy and distribute the handout at parent meetings, send the handout home with students, post it on the school Web site in a section designed just for parents, or print it in the school newsletter that gets sent home.

**NOTES:**

# PARENT POWER

It's a fact. Parents are the single most important influence in the lives of our students. Here are some tips for increasing the positive power parents have to help their children:

- Provide a high level of love, support, and positive words through day-to-day family life.

- Support and cultivate other adult relationships so that children receive support from three or more nonparent adults.

- Encourage community involvement so children feel that adults in the community value them and trust them enough to give them useful roles in the community.

- Provide children with a sense of safety at home, at school, and in the neighborhood.

- Establish clear rules and consequences and monitor children's whereabouts.

- Model positive, responsible behavior and peaceful conflict resolution.

- Maintain high expectations and encourage children to do well.

- Encourage children to be involved in sports and clubs and in activities in a religious institution.

- Make time spent at home appealing as a way to minimize the amount of time children are out with friends "with nothing special to do."

- Work with children to firm up their commitment to learning so that they are motivated to do well in school and do at least one hour of homework every school day.

- Help children bond with and care about their school.

- Model how and encourage children to read for pleasure.

- Help children develop positive values, demonstrated when they help others, promote equality, act on convictions, tell the truth, and accept personal responsibility.

- Teach children to believe it is important not to be sexually active as teenagers or to use alcohol or other drugs.

- Help children learn to plan ahead and make choices.

- Create opportunities for children to develop empathy and friendship skills and to become comfortable with people whose cultural/ racial/ethnic backgrounds are different from their own.

- Talk to children about reasons and ways to resist negative peer pressure and dangerous situations.

- Do everything you can to nurture children's self-esteem, sense of purpose, and positive view of their personal future.

**69**

# HOME LEARNING

> **KEY USER/S**
> Teachers
>
> **ASSET CATEGORY**
> Support
>
> **ASSETS ADDRESSED**
> #1, Family Support
> #2, Positive Family Communication
> #6, Parent Involvement in Schooling

## KEEP THIS IN MIND

Parents and guardians can do a great deal to reinforce what their children learn in school. Teachers can draw on parental support by letting parents know what the students are studying and how parents can help or get involved. Often all parents need is some idea of what their children are learning and how, specifically, they can help.

## HOW TO USE THIS HANDOUT

The handout helps teachers reach out to parents and guardians by asking for their support of extra-credit learning opportunities outside school.

Here are some other ways to involve parents and guardians in their children's education:

- Send regular letters home to parents telling them what their children are studying.

- Suggest specific ways parents can help with at-home learning. This might include visiting the library, museum, science or natural history center, or art gallery.

- Read together.

- Watch PBS, Animal Planet, the History Channel, a foreign film, or a documentary.

- Offer extra credit for students to write a short essay about what they learned and ask parents to sign off on it.

- Invite parents to come into the classroom to share what they know about a topic being studied in the classroom.

- Acknowledge parental involvement at parent-teacher conferences or by sending a brief note home with the student.

- Invite parents to help students surf the Internet to research topics and locate fun and interesting resources and information.

- Invite parents to work with children on projects such as history day presentations or special assignments that involve art or other media or drama.

# HOME LEARNING

Dear Parent/Guardian:

We all know that learning doesn't end when students leave the classroom. Your child has the opportunity to earn extra credit this semester by completing at least _____ hours of learning in addition to regularly assigned homework. This can range from community service to visiting the local library.

**Here are a few ideas that relate to this year's course of study:**

Please encourage your child to take advantage of this opportunity! When he or she has successfully completed this activity, please fill out the form below and turn it in to

_____ by _____.

(Name of teacher/staff member)                                    (Date)

**70**

_____ has earned extra credit for:

(Name of student)

(Student can write or draw a picture of what he or she accomplished below.)

_____          _____

(Student's signature)                                (Date)

_____          _____

(Parent's signature)                                (Date)

**70**

# SUMMER BRAINPOWER

**KEY USER/S**
Teachers, parents, guardians

**ASSET CATEGORY**
Support

**ASSETS ADDRESSED**
#1, Family Support
#2, Positive Family Communication
#6, Parent Involvement in Schooling

## KEEP THIS IN MIND

Summer is a time for fun, sun, and sometimes too much distance between learning intervals. Teachers can draw on parents to help students continue to flex their brains so that they can maintain the gains they've made during the previous school year.

## HOW TO USE THIS HANDOUT

Use the handout to structure summer learning for parents and students. Let parents know what topics you would like the students to address during the summer and give them some suggestions for how they might help the students stay on top of a particular subject. Include a letter explaining what this type of activity will help students accomplish.

**NOTES:**

71

# SUMMER BRAINPOWER

Date _____

Student's Name _____     Adviser _____

### SUMMER LEARNING GOALS

1. _____

2. _____

3. _____

### SUMMER ASSIGNMENTS

1. _____

2. _____

3. _____

### SUGGESTIONS FOR COMPLETING SUMMER ASSIGNMENTS

1. _____

2. _____

3. _____

**HOW PARENTS CAN HELP**

1. _____

2. _____

3. _____

Other help provided:




At the start of the next school year, please have the student turn this form in to:  (Post this form someplace where it won't get lost, like your refrigerator.)




Our child completed the work described under "Summer Assignments." We helped in the ways suggested above.


_____          _____

(Parent's Signature)                              (Date)

From *Pass It On at School! Activity Handouts for Creating Caring Schools,* copyright © 2003 by Search Institute; 612-376-8955; 800-888-7828; www.search-institute.org. This handout may be reproduced for educational, noncommercial uses only (with this copyright line). All rights reserved.

# OUTSIDE THE SCHOOL

## (COMMUNITY PARTNERSHIPS)

# CARING BY SHARING

**KEY USER/S**
School community, school commu-nity partnerships

**ASSET CATEGORY**
Support, Empowerment, Boundar-ies and Expectations

**ASSETS ADDRESSED**
#4, Caring Neighborhood
#7, Community Values Youth
#14, Adult Role Models
#16, High Expectations

## KEEP THIS IN MIND

Community business owners and organization leaders have much to contribute to asset build-ing in schools. Such individuals can contribute to the positive identity of students by sharing their expertise and information about career pathways and skills.

Schools can form partnerships with community businesses and organizations to provide mentorship opportunities for students. That may take the form of employees volunteering some time each month to spend at the school with students or youth going out and connecting one-on-one with adults.

Student-community mentor relationships are powerful asset-building tools and can give stu-dents positive role models and high expecta-tions. Young people also benefit from individual adult attention and gain a sense of what their future might hold.

## HOW TO USE THIS HANDOUT

The handout is a mentor-student "contract" that spells out the roles and responsibilities of each party.

## NOTES:

# CARING BY SHARING

## MENTORSHIP COMMITMENT

As the mentor, I agree to do the following:

1.  Participate in setting expectations for when, where, and how long we'll meet.
2.  Contact the student in advance if I can't meet with her or him and set up an alternative time to get together.
3.  Work with the student to determine what skills the student will gain from this relationship.
4.  Talk about the attitudes and behaviors we expect from each other.
5.  Share information about why I chose my career and how I prepared for it.
6.  Share with my student the traits and attitudes I believe make for success in the workplace.
7.  Celebrate the student's achievements and successes.

Mentor's Signature _____ Date _____

## STUDENT COMMITMENT

As the student, I agree to do the following:

1.  Participate in setting expectations for when, where, and how long we meet.
2.  Contact my mentor in advance if I can't meet with her or him, and set up an alternative time to get together.
3.  Tell my mentor what I hope to gain from the mentorship.
4.  Talk about the attitudes and behaviors we expect from each other.
5.  Be prepared to ask questions about my mentor's career choice.
6.  Keep an open mind and willingness to learn new things.

Student's Signature _____ Date _____

# EXPANDING BOUNDARIES

**KEY USER/S**
School staff, student organizations

**ASSET CATEGORY**
Empowerment, Positive values

**ASSETS ADDRESSED**
#7, Community Values Youth
#9, Service to Others
#26, Caring
#30, Responsibility

## KEEP THIS IN MIND

School communities can be expanded into the community at large. Involving students in community activities provides the chance for authentic learning. It also creates a rich set of opportunities for building assets that will empower students through service work and bolster positive values.

## HOW TO USE THIS HANDOUT

The following checklist for expanding school connections and learning opportunities into the larger community is meant to get the juices going. Use these examples as you brainstorm ideas that fit your particular school/community situation. Give all members of your school community a chance to think about and contribute ideas—you never know where the best ideas are hiding! Distribute the handout at staff meetings, in classrooms and after-school programs, and to members of clubs and sports teams. Make sure all young

people, including challenged and special education students, contribute. Ideas can come from anywhere, so don't forget the office, custodial, and security staff as well as food service workers, school bus drivers, parents, and volunteers.

Here are some ways in which students have been able to learn through connections with the larger community beyond the school:

*   **Mentoring.** Businesses in the community provide adult mentors for students.

*   **Service-learning.** Students work in community agencies that provide human services.

*   **Committee work.** Students participate on committees, councils, or standing boards that oversee community activities.

*   **Direct service.** Students join with community professionals to work with senior citizens, children, the humane society, and other groups to provide needed services.

# EXPANDING BOUNDARIES

**How can our school make the community better for everyone who lives and works here?**

Do you have an idea about how students and staff at our school can get involved and make the community better? Tell us your idea!

Do you know of a person, group, or organization in the community that could use the help of our students?

Can you think of ways for students to connect with the community beyond our school?

1.

2.

3.

What would you like to do out in the larger community? Are there any people or groups you'd like to help or work with? If so, who? Which groups?

# PASS IT ON **AT SCHOOL!** ———————————
## Activity Handout 73

Is there a person, business, or group you would like to come to the school to help out? If so, who?


What would you like them to do for/with our students?

# WE BELIEVE IN YOU(TH)!

**KEY USER/S**
School community, school/community partnerships

**ASSET CATEGORY**
Boundaries and Expectations, Social Competencies, Positive Identity

**ASSETS ADDRESSED**
#14, Adult Role Models
#16, High Expectations
#32, Planning and Decision Making
#40, Positive View of Personal Future

## KEEP THIS IN MIND

Most teenagers go to work at some point in their high school career, and those early work experiences begin to shape their attitudes, behavior, and competence in the work world for the rest of their lives. Schools can encourage employers to develop an asset-building mission that lets students know that they are appreciated and respected in the workplace.

## HOW TO USE THIS HANDOUT

The handout serves as a "mission statement" for employers and can be posted in a prominent place for everyone to see. Here's a real-life example of how one business made asset building a top priority:

## Fast-Food Restaurant Builds Assets and a Healthier Community

IN HARTFORD, KENTUCKY, the local McDonald's sounds more like a community center than a fast-food restaurant. Its secret? The store's owners are strong supporters of asset building and the local Healthy Communities • Healthy Youth initiative, Together We Care.

"There are so many ways that businesses can be useful in the community," says Valorie Tanner, who owns the restaurant with her husband, Vincent. Tanner says it wasn't hard to see the benefits of getting involved in the initiative's efforts, and she has been on board from the start. "We just thought it was time for us to do more for the community."

Here is a look at some of the ways this McDonald's is building assets:

- Every Tuesday morning, the restaurant sponsors a project that invites local high school students to read to preschool students in conjunction with the school district's "Read to Succeed" program. "We wanted to provide kids the opportunity to spend time with older kids," says Tanner. "Hopefully, this will

*cont.* ▶

be a way to get kids hooked on reading." The activity will take place in the restaurant's new Play Place area.

- With the Green and Growing Award, the restaurant recognizes the hard work of students in 1st to 6th grade. Teachers nominate the recipient who has made the most effort to improve and the young person is presented with a certificate for a free meal at McDonald's with her or his family.

- During the high school's fall dances and on holidays such as Valentine's Day, the restaurant offers candlelight dinners to give teenagers on a tight budget an alternative to more expensive restaurants. "We light candles, dim the lights, and act like a more full-service restaurant for a few hours," says Tanner.

- During February, which is Love My Bookmobile Month, the bookmobile parks in the restaurant's parking lot and offers an hour-long program full of stories and fun to youth participants. The youth are then invited to explore the bookmobile and have a snack, courtesy of McDonald's.

Story adapted from "Rising stars shine: Fast-food restaurant serves up more than french fries in Hartford, Kentucky," by Kalisha Davis. Found in *Assets: The Magazine of Ideas for Healthy Communities and Healthy Youth*, Autumn 2001.

# WE BELIEVE IN YOU(TH)!

We believe in **YOUR** ability to succeed in life.

## Here are the things that we commit to as your employer:

- Providing a supportive place to work and learn
- Respecting all staff
- Having fun! (At least as much fun as we can at work. ☺)

## Here are some ways that we'd like to help you be successful:

- Giving you time to do homework–Check in about important assignments at school or family activities so that we can make schedule adjustments. (Don't wait until the last minute!)

- Helping you learn something new–Is there something you'd like to find out more about around here? Ask us for more information.

- Making the community a better place for everyone–If there's something that you think is important, such as homelessness, the environment, or hunger, make a suggestion for how our workplace might help.

## Thanks for being a part of our team!

What type of suggestions do you have? Write them here: